Infrastructure as Code with OpenTofu

A perfect Terraform alternative to manage compute, storage, networking and other infrastructure resources

Tyran Vosk

Published by: GitforGits

Publisher: Sonal Dhandre

www.gitforgits.com

support@gitforgits.com

Printed in India

First Printing: December 2024

ISBN: 978-81-979504-3-8

Cover Design by: Kitten Publishing

Prologue

When I first got into cloud infrastructure, everyone was talking about Terraform. It was a total favorite among DevOps professionals. Its strong capabilities for managing IaC made it an essential tool. But as time went on, I started noticing that a lot of my peers and the DevOps community were getting pretty worried about the growing costs of Terraform. The licensing costs, along with the overhead of managing its extensive ecosystem, were starting to be a big deal for organizations trying to optimize their budgets without sacrificing quality of their infrastructure. I remember a lot of developers being frustrated about the hidden costs of Terraform. It was really good, but the price was too high, especially for startups and small to medium-sized businesses that don't have a lot of money. This frustration made me want to look for other options that could get the same, if not better, results without the high price tag. My research brought me to OpenTofu, which is an open-source tool that seemed like a good fit. It was flexible, cost-efficient, and had a solid community.

OpenTofu looked like it could be the answer, offering a solid alternative that could make infrastructure management more accessible to everyone. It worked well with Terraform configurations, so the transition wouldn't be hard. Teams could adopt it without completely overhauling their workflows. What I liked most was that OpenTofu was all about keeping IaC easy and cheap, which is exactly what modern developers want. As I learned more about OpenTofu, I got really excited. It's got awesome features, and there's a great community supporting it. It was clear to me that OpenTofu wasn't just another tool — it was a movement towards more sustainable and inclusive infrastructure management. It's like a game-changer because you can cut costs while keeping deployment capabilities the same or even boost them. I realized that mastering OpenTofu could empower developers to build, manage, and scale their infrastructures with greater autonomy and confidence. That's what motivated me to write this book and share my knowledge and experiences.

"Infrastructure as Code with OpenTofu" was born out of a passion to give cloud and DevOps professionals the skills they need to harness the full potential of OpenTofu. Whether you're a seasoned Terraform user looking to save some cash or a newbie eager to dive into IaC with a powerful tool, this book's got you covered. You'll learn practical, hands-on techniques to make the switch from Terraform to OpenTofu as smoothly as possible. You'll learn how to automate deployments, manage secrets securely, and integrate third-party tools like GitHub Actions to improve your infrastructure management practices. By switching to OpenTofu, you'll not only save on operational costs but also help foster a more collaborative and transparent infrastructure ecosystem.

Let's jump into the world of OpenTofu and see how it can transform the way you handle infrastructure as code. We'll tackle the challenges, celebrate the wins, and build a solid foundation for a future where cloud infrastructure management is more efficient and cost-effective.

Content

Preface ... *xi*

GitforGits ... *xii*

Acknowledgement ... *xiii*

Chapter 1: Introduction to OpenTofu and IaC ... **14**

Introduction ... *15*

What is Infrastructure as Code? ... *15*
IaC in Software Development ... 15
Automated Provisioning with Codified Configurations ... 16
Managing Resources with Code ... 16
Enhancing Collaboration and Agility ... 16
Scalability and Consistency ... 16

Why OpenTofu? ... *17*
Terraform's Dominant Role ... 17
OpenTofu as a Best Alternative ... 18
Features and Capabilities of OpenTofu ... 18
Familiar Command Structure ... 18
Open-Source Flexibility ... 18
Wide Provider Support ... 19
Module-Based Design ... 19
State Management ... 19
Drift Detection and Plan Workflow ... 19
Scalability and Automation ... 19
Smooth Migration Path ... 20
Community-Centric Innovation ... 20
Reduced Licensing Concerns ... 20
Integration with Existing Tooling ... 20
Modern IaC Principles ... 20
Balancing Familiarity and Innovation ... 21

Setting up OpenTofu ... *21*
Preparing the System for Installation ... 21
Installing OpenTofu Binary ... 22
Verifying Successful Installation ... 22
Basic Configuration Steps ... 22
Setting the Stage for Practical Use ... 23

Essential Concepts ... 23
Providers ... 23
Resources ... 24
Modules ... 24
State Management ... 24
Additional Elements ... 25

Summary ... 25

Chapter 2: Hands-on with OpenTofu Configurations ... 27

Introduction ... 28

Creating Configuration Files ... 28
Defining OpenTofu Configuration File ... 28
Writing a Simple Configuration ... 28
Introducing a Sample Book Project ... 29

Understanding Providers ... 30
Defining a Provider in OpenTofu ... 30
Authenticating with AWS ... 30
Working with Multiple Providers ... 31
Validating the Provider Setup ... 31
Adding Providers to Book Publishing Project ... 32

Declaring Resources ... 32
Declaring an EC2 Instance ... 32
Declaring an S3 Bucket ... 33
Referencing Provider Details ... 33
Combining Multiple Resources ... 34

Basic Plan and Apply Workflow ... 34
Previewing Changes with Plan ... 35
Executing Apply Step ... 35
Observing Workflow in our Book Publishing Project ... 35

Summary ... 36

Chapter 3: Exploring OpenTofu for Applications ... 37

Introduction ... 38

Core Components of App ... 38
Compute Requirements ... 38
Storage Requirements ... 38
Networking Requirements ... 39

Mapping Infrastructure to OpenTofu ... 39
Structuring Modules and Resources ... 39

Connecting Components 39
Summing Up 39

Organizing Codebase 40

Summary 41

Chapter 4: Advanced Resource Management 42

Introduction 43

Managing Resource Dependencies 43
Demonstrating Dependencies with a Publishing Application 43
Chaining Dependencies through Outputs 45
Avoiding Timing Conflicts 46

Resource Updates and Changes 46

Destroying Resources Safely 49

Customizing Resource Attributes 51

Summary 54

Chapter 5: Reusability with OpenTofu Modules 55

Introduction 56

Creating Your First Module 56

Input Variables in Modules 59

Outputs and Inter-Module Communication 63
Interconnecting Two Modules 64
Sample Program 65
Reading Outputs in other Resources 66
Testing and Verifying 66

Version Control for Modules 66

Summary 69

Chapter 6: State Management in OpenTofu 70

Introduction 71

Understanding State file 71
How State file track Infrastructure? 71
Local State Storage 71
Remote State Storage 72
Sample Program: Switching from Local to Remote 73

Handling State Drift 73

Discrepancies between Code and Real Infra ... 74
Changes Reconciliation ... 74
Sample Program: Bucket Policy Modified outside Code ... 74
Resolving Orphaned Resources ... 76
Ongoing Maintenance ... 76

State Locking ... 76
Why Locking in Multi-User Environments? ... 76
Defining Remote State Backend with Locking ... 77
Lock Prevention ... 78
Resolving Locking Conflicts ... 78
Sample Program: Simultaneous Changes ... 79

Summary ... 80

Chapter 7: Building and Deploying Apps ... 81

Introduction ... 82

Provisioning Compute Resources ... 82

Configuring Storage ... 85

Establishing Networking ... 86
Configuring Virtual Private Cloud ... 87
Define the VPC ... 87
Create Subnets ... 87
Internet Gateway and Route Tables ... 88
Setting up Security Groups ... 89
Define Security Groups ... 89
Attach Security Groups to EC2 ... 91
Integrating Networking Components ... 92
Create a NAT Gateway ... 92
Update Route Tables for Private Subnets ... 93
Additional Security Group Rules for enhanced Security ... 94
Scaling and Load Balancing ... 95

Integrating Database Services ... 98
Defining the RDS Instance ... 98
Creating a DB Subnet Group ... 99
Managing Database Credentials Securely ... 100
Enhancing Database Security with IAM Roles ... 101
Creating the Database Schema ... 103
Connecting Application to Database ... 104

Summary ... 104

Chapter 8: Organizing and Managing Workspaces ... 106

Introduction *107*

What Are Workspaces? *107*
Understanding Workspaces 107
Sample Program: Separating Environments with Workspaces 108
Initialize Default Workspace 108
Creating Separate Workspaces 108
Switching between Workspaces 108
Environment-specific Configurations 109
Managing Resources across Workspaces 110
Advanced Workspace Management 111
Using Modules with Workspaces 111
Dynamic Workspace Initialization 112

Switching between Workspaces *112*
Switching Workspaces Overview 113
Switching between Workspaces 113
Listing Available Workspaces 113
Creating a New Workspace 113
Selecting a Workspace 114
Automating Workspace Selection 114
Managing State across Workspaces 115
Understanding State Isolation 115
Viewing Current State 115
Moving Resources between Workspaces 115

Environment-specific Variables *116*
Introduction to Environment-specific Variables 116
Creating Workspace-specific Variable files 116
Applying Workspace-specific Variables 118
Integrating Variables into Resource Definitions 118
Managing Variable Files with Modules 121

Summary *124*

Chapter 9: Importing and Managing Existing Infrastructure **125**

Introduction *126*

Identifying Resources to Import *126*
Importance of Importing Resources 126
Inventory Existing Infrastructure 127
Gather Necessary Information for Each Resource 128
Prepare OpenTofu Configuration for Imported Resources 129
Document Dependencies and Order of Imports 130
Backup Current State and Configuration 131
Plan and Execute the Import 131
Reconcile and Validate the Import 133

Reconciliation Post-Import **134**
Understanding Reconciliation 134
Identify Configuration Mismatches 134
Update OpenTofu Configuration files 135
Utilizing 'opentofu fmt' and 'opentofu validate' 137
Automating Reconciliation Processes 137
Troubleshooting Reconciliation Issues 139

Updating State after Imports **141**
Review Imported Resources in the State File 141
Inspect Specific Resources 142
Validate and Format Configuration files 143
Final Plan to Confirm State Alignment 143
Commit Updated Configuration and State files 143

Summary **144**

Chapter 10: Deploying and Scaling Infrastructure **145**

Introduction **146**

Staging and Testing Deployments **146**
Deploying Infrastructure to Staging 146
Conducting Validation and Testing 147
Feedback-based Iteration 148
Prepare Promotion to Production 149
Implement Version Control 149
Setup CI/CD 149

Promoting Changes to Production **151**
Preparing the Production Workspace 151
Create a Production Workspace 151
Select the Production Workspace 151
Ensuring Configuration Consistency 151
Review and Update Variable Files 151
Update the Configuration files 152
Applying Configuration to Production 156
Implementing Rollback Plans 156

Scaling Infrastructure **157**
Figuring-out Scaling Requirements 158
OpenTofu Configuration for Auto Scaling 158
Define Launch Configuration 158
Create Auto Scaling Group 159
Configure Scaling Policies 160
Applying Scaling Configuration 163
Verifying Auto Scaling Configuration 165
Cost Management and Optimization 167

Use Spot Instances ... 167
Resource Tagging ... 167

Summary ... *168*

Chapter 11: Advanced Features and Automation ... 169

Introduction ... *170*

Automating Infrastructure Updates ... *170*

Overview ... 170

Setting up a CI/CD Pipeline ... 171

Storing Secrets in GitHub ... 171
Creating GitHub Actions Workflow ... 171
Committing and Pushing the Workflow ... 173
Testing the Automated Deployment ... 173

Managing Secrets in Configurations ... *174*

Best Practices for Managing Secrets ... 174

Strategies for Managing Secrets ... 175

Using Sensitive Variables ... 175
Integrating with Secret Management Services ... 177
Using GitHub Secrets with GitHub Actions ... 179
Encrypting State files ... 181
Integrating with HashiCorp Vault ... 182

Integrating Third-Party Tools ... *184*

Testing the Automated Deployment ... 184
Handling Failures and Rollbacks ... 185

Summary ... *185*

Epilogue ... *187*

Preface

This book is a must-have for cloud and DevOps professionals looking to take their infrastructure automation skills to the next level with OpenTofu — a game-changing tool that sets itself apart from other options like Terraform. It'll give you the hands-on techniques you need to streamline your infrastructure provisioning, deployment, and management, ensuring efficiency and consistency across environments. It'll take you through the ins and outs of OpenTofu, from setting up the initial configurations to deploying scalable and secure infrastructures. It teaches about how to automatically update infrastructure, how to create resources using loops and conditionals, and how to securely handle sensitive data. It teaches to work with GitHub Actions to improve deployment workflows so you can seamlessly integrate and deploy things. It also covers secret management, dynamic scaling, and integrating third-party tools to take OpenTofu's capabilities a step further.

It's basically a hands-on guide for folks with experience, showing how to replace those old IaC tools with OpenTofu, and it's packed with easy-to-practice examples. By the time you're done, you'll be able to automate complex infrastructure tasks, make sure everything is secure, and use your resources as efficiently as possible. This book is a must for anyone looking to up their infrastructure management game and adopt cutting-edge automation techniques using OpenTofu.

In this book you will learn to:

- Use OpenTofu's intuitive configurations to automate infrastructure deployments efficiently.
- Leverage loops and conditionals for scalable, repeatable resource provisioning.
- Securely manage sensitive data with environment variables and secret management services.
- Seamlessly integrate OpenTofu with GitHub Actions for streamlined CI/CD pipelines.
- Implement dynamic scaling strategies to handle varying application loads effectively.
- Utilize modules to create reusable, maintainable infrastructure components.
- Automate infrastructure updates to maintain consistency across multiple environments.
- Replace Terraform with OpenTofu to achieve cost-effective, flexible infrastructure management.

GitforGits

Prerequisites

Whether you're an experienced Terraform user trying to save some cash or a novice eager to dive into IaC with a solid tool, this book's got your back. You'll learn practical, hands-on techniques to make the switch from Terraform to OpenTofu as smoothly as possible.

Codes Usage

Are you in need of some helpful code examples to assist you in your programming and documentation? Look no further! Our book offers a wealth of supplemental material, including code examples and exercises.

Not only is this book here to aid you in getting your job done, but you have our permission to use the example code in your programs and documentation. However, please note that if you are reproducing a significant portion of the code, we do require you to contact us for permission.

But don't worry, using several chunks of code from this book in your program or answering a question by citing our book and quoting example code does not require permission. But if you do choose to give credit, an attribution typically includes the title, author, publisher, and ISBN. For example, "**Infrastructure as Code with OpenTofu** by **Tyran Vosk**".

If you are unsure whether your intended use of the code examples falls under fair use or the permissions outlined above, please do not hesitate to reach out to us at support@gitforgits.com.

We are happy to assist and clarify any concerns.

Acknowledgement

I owe a tremendous debt of gratitude to GitforGits, for their unflagging enthusiasm and wise counsel throughout the entire process of writing this book. Their knowledge and careful editing helped make sure the piece was useful for people of all reading levels and comprehension skills. In addition, I'd like to thank everyone involved in the publishing process for their efforts in making this book a reality. Their efforts, from copyediting to advertising, made the project what it is today.

Finally, I'd like to express my gratitude to everyone who has shown me unconditional love and encouragement throughout my life. Their support was crucial to the completion of this book. I appreciate your help with this endeavour and your continued interest in my career.

Chapter 1: Introduction to OpenTofu and IaC

Introduction

This chapter's all about the basics of Infrastructure as Code (IaC) and how OpenTofu is a useful, affordable way to put IaC into practice. When you adopt IaC principles, infrastructure management goes from manual, error-prone processes to automated, consistent, and repeatable workflows. You will see a shift in how infrastructure management is done. With OpenTofu's open-source platform, DevOps pros can keep things flexible and scalable while managing infrastructure efficiently.

To get started, you will need to set up OpenTofu on your system. You will walk through the steps to install, configure, and verify that it's up and running. This basic setup will show you the tools and workflows needed to manage your infrastructure as code using OpenTofu's simple syntax and commands. We will then explore the key concepts of OpenTofu, like providers, resources, modules, and state management. These concepts are the building blocks for all IaC configurations, so you will be able to describe, provision, and manage infrastructure components programmatically. By the time you are done with this chapter, you will get a clear understanding of what OpenTofu offers and how it fits into a DevOps workflow. That way, you will be all set to dive deeper into hands-on infrastructure management.

What is Infrastructure as Code?

IaC has fundamentally transformed how modern software applications are built, tested, and deployed. In traditional setups, provisioning infrastructure—servers, databases, networking components, and more—required manual intervention, often leading to inconsistencies, delays, and human errors. With the advent of IaC, these processes have become automated and programmatically manageable, enabling teams to focus more on development and less on infrastructure concerns.

IaC in Software Development

As software development cycles have shortened with the rise of Agile methodologies and DevOps practices, the need for rapid, reliable, and repeatable infrastructure provisioning has grown. CI/CD pipelines demand environments that can be provisioned on demand, ensuring that code is tested in isolated, consistent setups before reaching production. IaC addresses this by providing a way to define and deploy infrastructure using code, ensuring consistency across development, staging, and production environments.

Furthermore, IaC integrates seamlessly into existing software development workflows. Just as developers track application code changes through version control systems like Git, IaC enables tracking infrastructure changes, fostering better collaboration among teams. This has become particularly significant as organizations adopt cloud-native approaches, requiring infrastructure to scale dynamically based on workload demands. The ability to programmatically scale resources has not only reduced operational overhead but also aligned infrastructure management with the fast-paced evolution of software applications.

Automated Provisioning with Codified Configurations

At its core, IaC replaces manual provisioning processes with codified configurations. These configurations act as blueprints for infrastructure, specifying what resources are required, how they are interconnected, and what attributes they should possess. For example, a configuration file might declare an EC2 instance with a specific instance type, attached storage, and networking rules. When executed, IaC tools translate these configurations into actual infrastructure components, provisioning them on the desired platform.

Automation through IaC eliminates the repetitive and error-prone tasks associated with manual setup. For instance, setting up a test environment with multiple interdependent services often involves numerous steps, each susceptible to human error. IaC automates these tasks, ensuring each deployment adheres to predefined parameters. Whether provisioning a single server or a complex multi-tier application, the process is consistent and repeatable, reducing the likelihood of misconfigurations.

Managing Resources with Code

One of IaC's defining characteristics is its ability to treat infrastructure resources as code. Just as developers write, review, and maintain application code, infrastructure configurations can be version-controlled, peer-reviewed, and iteratively improved. Through IaC, resources are not only provisioned but also managed throughout their lifecycle. Updates to configurations automatically propagate to the corresponding resources, ensuring the infrastructure evolves in sync with application requirements. Similarly, decommissioning unused resources becomes as simple as removing their definitions from the codebase, promoting efficient resource utilization and cost management.

Enhancing Collaboration and Agility

IaC plays a pivotal role in bridging the gap between development and operations teams, a core tenet of the DevOps movement. By codifying infrastructure, developers and operations teams work with a shared language, minimizing misunderstandings and ensuring alignment in goals. Teams can collaboratively design, review, and implement infrastructure changes, leading to faster delivery cycles and fewer bottlenecks.

Additionally, IaC enables experimentation and innovation by making it easier to create and tear down environments. Developers can test new features or configurations without fear of affecting production systems, as isolated environments can be spun up quickly using the same underlying configurations. This agility has become indispensable in modern software development, where iterative improvement is the norm.

Scalability and Consistency

As organizations grow, so do their infrastructure needs. Scaling applications to meet increasing demands often requires provisioning additional resources, configuring load balancers, and adjusting network settings. Without IaC, managing such growth can become unmanageable, especially when consistency across environments is crucial.

IaC ensures that scaling operations remain predictable and reliable. By declaring infrastructure in code, scaling up or down involves modifying configurations and applying those changes. For instance, adding more application servers to handle increased traffic is as straightforward as updating a resource count in the configuration file. IaC tools then handle the actual provisioning and integration of these resources, reducing the operational burden.

Moreover, IaC ensures that scaling efforts do not introduce inconsistencies. Whether provisioning one server or a hundred, the configurations ensure that each resource adheres to the same specifications, maintaining uniformity across deployments.

The codified nature of IaC also aligns with disaster recovery and high availability goals. In the event of failures, entire environments can be recreated using the same configurations, minimizing downtime and ensuring business continuity. This capability has been particularly valuable for organizations operating in highly competitive or regulated industries, where system availability and reliability are paramount.

Why OpenTofu?

Terraform's Dominant Role

Many professionals first encounter IaC through the Terraform tool created by HashiCorp. This platform gained widespread acceptance for its ability to define cloud and on-premises resources using a flexible configuration language. Individuals and organizations embraced Terraform because it offered a single workflow for multiple providers, from AWS and Azure to GCP and other specialized services. By describing infrastructure in files rather than manual scripts, teams found it simpler to version-control configurations, collaborate effectively, and reduce misconfigurations. Over time, Terraform became a near-default option for many DevOps and cloud practitioners, owing to its straightforward approach and robust provider ecosystem.

In addition, Terraform's modular structure and community-driven modules contributed to its popularity. Many DevOps teams leveraged pre-built modules to accelerate project timelines without reinventing the wheel for every environment. The tool's support for plan and apply steps brought clarity to changes before they were made, reducing the uncertainty around updates to infrastructure. Furthermore, Terraform integrated well with continuous integration and deployment systems, enabling end-to-end automation of provisioning. These characteristics made it a pillar of modern infrastructure management, especially in organizations seeking to streamline operations and adopt best approaches for resource lifecycle management.

Despite these advantages, certain limitations began to emerge in practice. Some teams faced constraints around enterprise features, additional licensing, and potential friction when scaling beyond a basic deployment. The cost factor for advanced features also became an obstacle, especially for smaller organizations or those looking to experiment without significant financial commitments. Over time, the open-source community noticed a growing need for an alternative that would align with the same configuration language and workflow, but with fewer restrictions. This realization led to the emergence of OpenTofu, viewed by many as a promising path forward for those who prefer a more open, cost-conscious option.

OpenTofu as a Best Alternative

OpenTofu stepped into the IaC landscape to address concerns around Terraform's licensing and proprietary features. It is designed to resemble Terraform in command structure and language, which makes transitions smoother. Instead of requiring users to adapt entirely new workflows or learn different syntax, OpenTofu retains much of what Terraform practitioners already know. This allows teams to migrate configurations and skills quickly, avoiding the steep learning curve often associated with a new tool.

Another notable aspect is OpenTofu's open-source nature, which leads to transparent development processes and community collaboration. Individuals can contribute, request features, or review the codebase without barriers. This fosters trust, especially for those who wish to keep their workflows free from vendor lock-in or licensing surprises. For smaller teams that might only provision a handful of resources at a time, running an open-source tool without hidden fees can be quite appealing. For larger enterprises, the flexibility to tailor the tool's functionality to internal use cases can also be a determining factor.

Being a best alternative means more than just matching Terraform's features—it involves actively innovating in areas where there is room for improvement. They aim to maintain the same level of compatibility with major cloud services, ensuring that AWS, Azure, GCP, and other providers remain accessible through the new tool. Ultimately, for teams that appreciate the structural patterns of Terraform but wish to avoid proprietary elements, OpenTofu stands out as a compelling choice.

Features and Capabilities of OpenTofu

Familiar Command Structure

Practitioners who have been using Terraform find many parallels, including commands for initializing, planning, and applying changes. This similarity reduces confusion during adoption, because existing skill sets transfer easily. Individuals can keep using a command-line experience that feels familiar, yet discover additional enhancements that OpenTofu introduces.

Open-Source Flexibility

The project is entirely open source, which promotes transparency. Community members can review the code, provide feedback, or propose changes. This collaborative ecosystem fosters a sense of ownership among users, who can help shape the tool's direction. In practical terms, this means bug fixes or new features can move faster when guided by community needs rather than a single company's roadmap.

Wide Provider Support

Much like Terraform, OpenTofu interacts with a broad range of providers, spanning major cloud platforms to specialized services. An AWS provider might handle EC2 instances, S3 buckets, and IAM policies, while an Azure provider could manage resources in Azure Resource Manager. This aligns well with multi-cloud strategies, because individuals can define all resources in one place. Where a provider does not exist, the community often steps in to build and maintain it, ensuring coverage grows over time.

Module-Based Design

Modules remain a key piece of this tool's structure, allowing teams to encapsulate common configurations into reusable components. For example, a standardized VPC module might define subnets, route tables, and security rules. Another module might handle application servers, from instance creation to load balancing. By packaging these definitions as modules, teams can maintain consistency and reduce repetition, while also enforcing certain standards across different environments.

State Management

Similar to Terraform, OpenTofu tracks the state of infrastructure, knowing which resources exist and their relationships. This state management ensures that changes apply only where needed, preventing accidental overwrites or unpredictable deployments. One can store state files locally or remotely, depending on organizational preferences. Remote storage often includes locking mechanisms that guard against simultaneous updates.

Drift Detection and Plan Workflow

The "plan" command is integral to the tool's workflow, offering a preview of what changes will be applied before they happen. If resources in a cloud environment drift from their declared configurations—perhaps due to manual edits in the console—the plan step highlights these discrepancies. Correcting drift then becomes as simple as reapplying the appropriate code, restoring the environment to its desired state.

Scalability and Automation

Automation sits at the heart of any IaC tool, and OpenTofu is no exception. Pipelines built for testing, building, and deploying code can easily add an infrastructure provisioning step. From simple command-line scripts to sophisticated CI/CD workflows, the application of OpenTofu configurations remains straightforward. This helps organizations swiftly spin up new environments, whether for development, staging, or production, and tear them down just as quickly when they are no longer required. The result is an agile ecosystem that can pivot rapidly in response to new business needs.

Smooth Migration Path

For those already invested in Terraform, the developers of OpenTofu have emphasized compatibility. In many cases, terraform configurations can function in OpenTofu with minimal adjustments. That means existing knowledge, scripts, and modules often transfer directly. This migration path appeals to teams that wish to explore a different approach without discarding the progress or skill sets built around Terraform over time.

Community-Centric Innovation

OpenTofu's open nature and mission promote a culture of collaboration. When a new feature is needed, users have the option to request or implement it. The maintainers welcome feedback, and the roadmap is shaped by real-world usage rather than a top-down directive. This means features that matter most to the broader user base tend to get priority. Over time, such an ecosystem can produce innovative capabilities that outpace less flexible solutions.

Reduced Licensing Concerns

Licensing constraints or expenses might deter teams from experimenting with certain functionalities in other tools. By contrast, OpenTofu is free to use, aligning with the open-source philosophy of accessible technology. Individuals and organizations can adopt it without fear of hidden costs, paywalls, or seats-based limitations. This fosters an environment where DevOps culture is truly democratized—experimentation thrives without tying budgets to specialized enterprise add-ons.

Integration with Existing Tooling

Beyond provisioning, teams often employ a range of complementary tools for logging, monitoring, and security scanning. OpenTofu can be embedded into these existing workflows just as Terraform can, thanks to its modular design and consistent syntax. Whether hooking into a GitHub Actions pipeline, a GitLab CI/CD job, or a custom automation framework, the process remains simple and clear. This ensures that adopting OpenTofu does not introduce friction with established practices.

Modern IaC Principles

As DevOps evolves, new concepts continue to emerge. OpenTofu is built around current IaC principles that emphasize codification, automation, repeatability, and version control. These pillars reflect the way organizations want to manage resources, especially when dealing with microservices, container orchestrators, or complex multi-cloud deployments. By reinforcing these fundamentals, OpenTofu remains relevant in an ever-evolving ecosystem.

Balancing Familiarity and Innovation

OpenTofu mirrors many of Terraform's familiar elements, but it also opens the door to new possibilities. The focus on community-driven enhancements can lead to features that directly address user demands. Without proprietary gates, there is a sense of freedom in how far the tool can go, especially in addressing corner cases or specialized use scenarios that might not otherwise receive attention.

The choice between Terraform and OpenTofu often depends on organizational priorities. Some prefer the comfort of a well-known tool with enterprise offerings, while others seek a truly open environment that encourages experimentation. For many individuals, adopting OpenTofu is less about rejecting Terraform and more about supporting the free, community-oriented path. By doing so, they join a collective effort to shape an IaC experience that remains flexible, transparent, and continually refined.

Terraform's legacy and continued dominance in the IaC space are undeniable. However, OpenTofu provides a refreshing alternative for those drawn to open-source values and cost efficiency. As infrastructure and software development keep evolving, a tool that integrates seamlessly with established processes while encouraging collaborative innovation can have significant appeal. This is especially evident as more teams explore multi-cloud strategies, container orchestration, and ephemeral test environments, all of which benefit from a straightforward IaC tool that welcomes community contributions.

Setting up OpenTofu

Preparing the System for Installation

Often, a Linux environment includes a package manager that makes it easy to set up new tools. OpenTofu's installation requires a few utilities, such as **`wget`** and **`unzip`**, to download and extract the binary. If these utilities are missing, a command sequence such as the following may be used on a Debian-based system:

```
sudo apt-get update
sudo apt-get install -y wget unzip
```

One might also create a dedicated directory to store upcoming OpenTofu configurations, ensuring each project remains separate and properly organized. For instance, a command like:

```
mkdir -p ~/opentofu-projects
```

helps gather everything in one place. This arrangement simplifies handling multiple files and modules as learning progresses.

Installing OpenTofu Binary

Most individuals prefer a direct download of the precompiled binary. A typical release filename might look like **opentofu_<version>_linux_amd64.zip**. After identifying the correct version from the official download source, commands similar to the following can be executed:

```
wget https://gitforgits.com/opentofu_<version>_linux_amd64.zip
sudo unzip opentofu_<version>_linux_amd64.zip -d
/usr/local/bin
```

If the system does not automatically assign execute permissions, a quick check can be done with:

```
ls -l /usr/local/bin/opentofu
```

and if needed:

```
sudo chmod +x /usr/local/bin/opentofu
```

Placing the binary in **/usr/local/bin** allows the operating system to recognize **opentofu** as an executable command from any directory. Alternatively, individuals who do not have root privileges can extract the binary to a custom folder (for instance, **$HOME/bin**) and update the **$PATH** to reference that location.

Verifying Successful Installation

The key to testing your installation is to make sure that everything in your environment is working and working together. An easy way to verify this is to:

```
opentofu version
```

A successful output confirms that OpenTofu is recognized and ready to parse Infrastructure as Code configurations. If the command cannot be found, double-check that **/usr/local/bin** (or whichever directory was chosen) is part of the **$PATH** environment variable. For example, if one chose **$HOME/bin**, adding the following line to **~/.bashrc** or **~/.zshrc** might be necessary:

```
export PATH="$PATH:$HOME/bin"
```

Once the file is saved and the shell is reloaded (for example, using **source ~/.bashrc**), OpenTofu should become accessible without manual path specification.

Basic Configuration Steps

OpenTofu interacts with various providers, so ensuring valid credentials is important before proceeding to more advanced topics. For instance, when working with AWS, one might set the following environment variables:

```
export AWS_ACCESS_KEY_ID="YOUR_ACCESS_KEY_ID"
export AWS_SECRET_ACCESS_KEY="YOUR_SECRET_ACCESS_KEY"
export AWS_DEFAULT_REGION="us-east-1"
```

Alternatively, some opt for the AWS CLI configuration system, storing credentials in **~/.aws/credentials** and reusing them seamlessly within OpenTofu. No extensive configuration beyond this is strictly required at this point, but having credentials ready sidesteps delays when the time arrives to apply real deployments.

Setting the Stage for Practical Use

With OpenTofu installed, verified, and initial credentials in place, the environment is nearly set for practical IaC exercises. A dedicated folder—such as **~/opentofu-projects**—can contain subfolders for different sets of resources, environment-specific files, or modules. For example:

```
cd ~/opentofu-projects
mkdir -p aws-basic-setup
```

Inside **aws-basic-setup**, future files like **main.tf** might declare resources or providers. This consistent layout simplifies file management, version control, and subsequent collaboration.

Essential Concepts

OpenTofu aligns with Infrastructure as Code principles by treating every component of a cloud or on-premises system as something definable in text-based configurations. These files capture specific details about each resource, ensuring that environments remain consistent and repeatable. The tool itself covers a range of important ideas, from providers that handle cloud interactions to modules that bundle related configuration.

They are as below:

Providers

A provider is responsible for connecting OpenTofu to external platforms or services. Each provider knows how to create, update, and remove resources on that platform. For instance, the AWS provider handles tasks such as launching EC2 instances or configuring S3 buckets. The code typically includes a block that specifies which provider is used and, if needed, the provider's version. Authentication data, such as credentials or tokens, is often stored separately for security. This approach lets the code remain flexible and portable because sensitive details do not appear in plain text. Multiple providers can coexist in one project, which is helpful when working with hybrid environments that span different services or clouds. By controlling provider versions, teams ensure consistent behavior, so new features or updates do not unexpectedly break the existing configurations.

Resources

Resources are the fundamental building blocks declared within the code. Each resource block indicates a specific infrastructure component, such as a virtual server, a storage bucket, or a database. Attributes within that block define details like capacity, region, network settings, and tags. Because each resource is declared in a file, version control systems can track changes and show how an environment evolves over time. If the code modifies a resource, OpenTofu calculates a plan to show what will change before proceeding. This helps prevent surprises during provisioning. In addition, resources can reference one another. A server resource, for instance, can connect to a subnet resource by using outputs from the subnet block. This lets one easily see how the infrastructure pieces relate to each other, promoting a more organized perspective on architecture.

Modules

Modules enhance reusability and maintainability by grouping multiple resources into a single logical container. They allow one to avoid writing repetitive code for each instance of a common pattern, such as a web server configuration or a network layout. A module typically includes input variables, output values, and resource declarations. Input variables let different environments or teams customize settings like instance type or network addresses, while output values provide references to items within the module, such as created resource IDs or endpoints. Teams often store modules in separate directories or external repositories, making them easy to share across multiple projects. When a module is updated—perhaps to improve security settings—those improvements can be applied wherever the module is used, avoiding manual edits across many locations.

State Management

State management distinguishes IaC tools like OpenTofu from mere configuration scripts. The state file records the real-world attributes of the resources under management, allowing the code to remain in sync with the actual environment. Whenever new resources are deployed, updated, or removed, the state file keeps track of those changes. If the state is stored locally, only one individual at a time can safely manage the environment, because a single local file might not accommodate concurrent modifications. Remote state storage, often using a cloud bucket or database, introduces locking to prevent collisions between multiple team members. This fosters collaboration, as all participants share a consistent view of existing infrastructure. Drift can occur when resources are altered outside the code, so state-aware workflows catch those differences and prompt adjustments to restore alignment.

Additional Elements

Variables and outputs are pivotal to flexible setups. Variables define parameters that may shift between environments, such as region names, instance sizes, or feature toggles. Instead of hardcoding these details, one can store them in separate files or pass them as command-line inputs. This method streamlines environment-specific configuration, so the same codebase can power development, staging, and production, with only variable files differing. Outputs, on the other hand, hand back important information from resources or modules, such as IP addresses or security group IDs, for use in other parts of the project. By employing these elements, the overall structure becomes more coherent.

Dependency management is also handled via references in the code. When one resource references attributes from another, OpenTofu infers the creation order. That ensures that, for instance, a route table is not attempted before the underlying subnet is available. This can extend across multiple modules, removing the burden of manually dictating the sequence of tasks.

Finally, workspaces or separate states can isolate environments. While variables differentiate certain aspects, distinct workspaces prevent overlap in resource definitions. This is practical for teams working on different phases of deployment or for parallel testing. Each workspace maintains its own state, so commands like plan and apply operate only on that environment. This alignment keeps dev, staging, and production in separate realms while still sharing similar modules and configurations.

By combining vendors, resources, modules and state management, OpenTofu provides a systematic way to define and monitor infrastructure. Those familiar with other IaC approaches will see similarities. However, the open source nature of this platform and its community-driven ethos sets it apart. Eventually, advanced features such as dynamic blocks or custom providers may be used, but they are built on the foundation described here.

Summary

This introductory chapter introduced you to the concept of managing infrastructure with code instead of manual configurations. You learned how Infrastructure as Code reduces inconsistencies and simplifies operations by putting every setting under version control. You saw how OpenTofu provides an open source path that mirrors many of Terraform's features while removing licensing barriers. The steps to install on Linux were provided, guiding you through downloading and unpacking a single binary, and verifying a successful command line install. You also learned about the benefits of remote state storage for collaborative projects, which prevents conflicts during simultaneous updates.

The chapter also emphasized the importance of providers, resources, and modules, and showed you how everything is connected under a maintained state file. You saw how each resource component, whether a server or a storage bucket, can be declared in reusable blocks for consistent deployments. This integrates seamlessly with modern CI/CD and Agile workflows, allowing infrastructure changes to evolve along with application code.

CHAPTER 2: HANDS-ON WITH OPENTOFU CONFIGURATIONS

Introduction

In this chapter, you will begin to learn how to create and structure configuration files that define basic resource attributes, providers, and any necessary variables. Each file will serve a different purpose, whether it is storing provider versions or listing the compute instances needed for a particular environment. This step provides a direct path to building confidence in OpenTofu's workflow, as everything from small experiments to more detailed projects can share a consistent structure.

Next, you will explore the role of providers in connecting your declarations to actual services. You will see how credentials are securely referenced and how each file points to the desired cloud platform or external system. This focus on providers lays the groundwork for declaring specific resources-whether a single server or a multi-node setup-by assigning names, sizes, and networking preferences. Finally, you apply what you have written through the Plan and Apply commands, which preview changes before you actually deploy them. Then you use apply to turn those definitions into reality. This cycle can be repeated to adjust resources, fix bugs, and refine settings, all of which pave the way for more sophisticated activities in the future.

Creating Configuration Files

Defining OpenTofu Configuration File

The first step is to create plain text configuration files that define the infrastructure elements to be added, changed, or deleted. These files contain essential details such as the selected provider, resource types, and attributes such as region, size, and optional tags. When you apply the configuration, OpenTofu processes each segment and interacts with the specified platform or service, provisioning resources that match your text-based definitions. You don't need a specialized development environment; a simple text editor or code editor will do. By organizing the code in a clear and readable way, you can easily understand and review what you are deploying.

When updates are required, the planning step previews the changes, and the final step applies them, bringing the changes to life. This workflow is flexible enough to support multiple cloud providers or custom platforms, allowing you to manage a variety of resources from a single command line interface. By storing these configuration files in a version control system, you can track changes, roll them back if necessary, or seamlessly collaborate with others. As your project grows, you can split configurations into separate files or use modules to better organize your infrastructure. Regardless of complexity, the basic idea remains the same: define your desired infrastructure in text to achieve a more streamlined and manageable deployment process.

Writing a Simple Configuration

We start by creating a small text file—perhaps named **`main.tf`**—where you define the provider and one basic resource. Since OpenTofu can manage various cloud platforms, you might specify a line or two that references a cloud provider like AWS, along with its version requirement. Then we declare a resource block, which might look something like this (adjusted for personal environment):

```
provider "aws" {
  region = "us-east-1"
}
resource "aws_instance" "basic_vm" {
  ami           = "ami-12345678"
  instance_type = "t2.micro"
}
```

When we save this file in a folder, we have our first explicit definition of a resource within OpenTofu. The **aws_instance** name indicates the resource type, while **"basic_vm"** is how we reference it in the code. Within that resource block, we detail the AMI to use and the size we want. Nothing else is required at this stage, though you can add optional tags or networking parameters later. We now confirm that our environment variables or credentials are set so that OpenTofu can authenticate. Once we run the commands to initialize and plan, the plan step should show that it intends to create one new EC2 instance. When you choose to proceed, OpenTofu will deploy that instance in your account. By structuring it in a single file, you keep it straightforward and can expand upon it as the need arises. This basic file will form the foundation, and you will see how it can be extended to multiple resources, varying providers, or more refined attributes that suit broader scenarios.

Introducing a Sample Book Project

You can imagine building a small application to publish and manage a catalog of electronic or print works. This project might include an EC2 instance to run a backend application, a database to store author details, and S3 buckets for manuscript files. You can ensure consistency across environments such as development, test, or production by encoding these components in OpenTofu configuration files. You can define the compute layer in one file and manage storage and networking in another. Over time, you might decide to reference these configurations in separate modules or keep everything in one file for simplicity, depending on your needs.

Initially, you may want to declare a single instance to familiarize yourself with the process. Later, you can expand by associating additional resources with that instance, such as subnets, security groups, and load balancers. The simplicity of this application concept-uploading manuscripts, organizing metadata, and distributing finished books-makes it an ideal example to demonstrate the incremental approach of Infrastructure as Code. Each action you take, from creating basic configuration files to integrating more advanced features, builds toward a functional system that runs reliably in the cloud. By keeping all references in text, you can track how your project evolves over time, introducing new features while ensuring that everything stays in line with the defined configurations.

Understanding Providers

Defining a Provider in OpenTofu

Providers are the link between your configuration code and actual platforms. You can integrate with AWS, Azure, or other environments under a single project. Each provider block specifies an external service and sets details such as region or version restrictions. For example, defining an AWS provider means specifying which region to target and where credentials are stored. The credentials can be retrieved from environment variables, from configuration files, or from a secure credential manager. Without a provider block, the system does not know what service is being addressed, so including it is essential for any meaningful deployment.

A minimal AWS configuration often looks like this:

```
provider "aws" {
  region  = "us-east-1"
  # Additional optional settings
}
```

Once saved in a file such as **provider.tf**, it aligns your local project with a specified region, ready for resource declarations.

Authenticating with AWS

When working with AWS, you might rely on environment variables like **AWS_ACCESS_KEY_ID** and **AWS_SECRET_ACCESS_KEY**. If environment variables are set, OpenTofu reads them by default. Another option is referencing a profile in the **~/.aws/credentials** file, which is often chosen when juggling multiple accounts or roles.

For instance, a credentials file might hold:

```
 [default]
aws_access_key_id = YOUR_KEY_ID
aws_secret_access_key = YOUR_SECRET_KEY
```

The provider block does not typically show these keys, preserving security. Once the file is configured or the environment variables are set, you can confirm everything by running commands like **opentofu plan** on a basic configuration. The plan step will show if it can read AWS settings.

Working with Multiple Providers

You can have interactions with multiple platforms within the same project. For example, one file might declare an AWS provider to handle virtual machines, while another file might reference a DNS service. Each provider block can share the same project structure, allowing a single command to manage all resources across multiple clouds. If you need to differentiate environments or manage separate accounts, you can label providers with aliases.

An alias might look like this

```
provider "aws" {
  alias  = "staging"
  region = "us-east-2"
}
provider "aws" {
  alias  = "production"
  region = "us-west-1"
}
```

When declaring a resource, reference the intended provider by name and alias, ensuring each resource deploys in the correct account or region.

Validating the Provider Setup

After defining providers, the next step is often initialization. A command like:

```
opentofu init
```

grabs any needed plugins or modules. If the provider is AWS, that plugin is downloaded so the system can communicate with the cloud platform. Once the init step completes, a simple plan command reveals whether the setup is recognized:

```
opentofu plan
```

If everything aligns, you see a plan output indicating zero changes or listing actions needed for the declared resources. If a mismatch occurs—like missing credentials—an error message might appear. Reviewing that feedback clarifies which part needs adjustment, whether it is an incorrect region or absent environment variables.

Adding Providers to Book Publishing Project

Since the sample project you envision might run on AWS, your code can contain an AWS provider block that references the appropriate region. Later, if a requirement arises to store images on another service or manage DNS via a separate provider, each new provider configuration can be added. One might place them in a single file or split them into multiple files for clarity. The overall objective is to maintain a clear understanding of which services your code can interact with. The presence of these blocks is what empowers each resource definition to come to life. If a resource references AWS, the AWS provider block ensures that calls go to the right APIs, shaped by any region or alias details you have outlined.

Providers do not provide a resource in and of themselves, but they do set the stage for resource definitions to occur. Specifying credentials, region, and possible aliases gives you control over the environment. This control is key as the project grows to include multiple environments - such as development, staging, and production - or even multiple cloud providers. Once vendors are defined, resource blocks reference them to create servers, storage, networking, and other infrastructure components. This layout keeps the entire system modular, so you can update or replace provider configurations without reworking each individual asset. When you change a provider block, a quick plan run shows the impact on resources, giving you visibility into any changes.

Declaring Resources

When we want to create or modify actual infrastructure, we rely on resource blocks within our OpenTofu configuration. Each block corresponds to a specific infrastructure component, defining attributes like size, type, and other details that shape how it will be provisioned. If you are using the AWS provider, resources typically have names like **aws_instance** or **aws_s3_bucket**, making it straightforward to tell them apart. After writing or editing these blocks, you run a plan to see how OpenTofu interprets your intentions, and then you apply them to bring the resources to life.

Declaring an EC2 Instance

A common starting point is to spin up a virtual machine in AWS. If you have already configured the AWS provider, you can write something like this in a **.tf** file:

```
resource "aws_instance" "my_ec2" {
  ami           = "ami-12345678"
  instance_type = "t2.micro"
  tags = {
    Name = "MyFirstEC2"
```

```
  }
}
```

Here, **aws_instance** indicates the resource type, and **"my_ec2"** is your chosen label. Inside the block, you specify the AMI you want, the instance type, and a few other properties as needed. After saving the file, you run:

```
opentofu plan
opentofu apply
```

The OpenTofu then deploys the instance using the AWS provider details. If you later want to increase its size, you change **instance_type** to something else, run the plan again, and see how that might affect the environment.

Declaring an S3 Bucket

Here, another resource might be a storage bucket for hosting files. If you want to create a bucket that can store data or logs, you add a separate block that looks like:

```
resource "aws_s3_bucket" "my_bucket" {
  bucket = "my-unique-bucket-name-123"
  acl    = "private"
}
```

When you apply, OpenTofu ensures the bucket is created in your specified region, as set by the AWS provider block. Naming uniqueness matters here. If the name is already taken globally, you might see an error indicating you need to pick a different name. Once the bucket is created, you can add more attributes if you wish, such as enabling versioning or configuring lifecycle rules. Any of these changes remain captured in the code, so if you ever remove this block, OpenTofu recognizes that the bucket is no longer desired and prompts you before deleting it.

Referencing Provider Details

Because these resources rely on the AWS provider, you do not need to restate region or credentials in each resource block. The provider you declared earlier supplies those settings automatically. If you have multiple providers or aliases, you can specify which one the resource should use by adding a provider reference.

Let us consider an example:

```
resource "aws_s3_bucket" "my_bucket" {
```

```
  provider = aws.my_alias
  bucket   = "my-other-bucket"
  acl      = "private"
}
```

In the above scenario, you ensure the resource is linked to the correct alias. This is how you keep different environments separate without confusion, especially if you store data for testing or production in distinct AWS accounts.

Combining Multiple Resources

A very important point for you and me too is that nothing stops us from placing multiple resource blocks in the same file. For instance, you can have an EC2 resource and an S3 bucket in one **.tf** file, grouped under relevant headings for clarity. Alternatively, you might split them across multiple files, like **ec2.tf** and **storage.tf**. Either way, OpenTofu reads every **.tf** file in the folder during the plan and apply steps, generating a single cohesive infrastructure plan. If any resources need to reference each other, you do that using output variables or direct references.

When referencing an EC2 instance ID within another resource, you might use something like:

```
resource "aws_eip" "my_ip" {
  instance = aws_instance.my_ec2.id
}
```

That reference instructs OpenTofu to attach an Elastic IP to the existing instance, ensuring it is known in the plan that the instance must exist first.

Let's say you want to set up an EC2 instance to handle the backend for a publishing application. That instance could run a simple server for receiving manuscript uploads. At the same time, you can set up an S3 bucket to store those files so authors can submit their work. Each part of the configuration describes a piece of that puzzle, and references can tie them together where relevant. If the instance needs an IAM role to upload to the bucket, you can add an IAM role resource, an IAM policy resource, and link them to the instance or bucket. Each time you add a resource block, you should verify it through a plan step. If you remove a resource block, the plan indicates that OpenTofu wants to destroy that resource. This makes it easy to see what's written in the code and what's actually there in the cloud.

Basic Plan and Apply Workflow

Previewing Changes with Plan

Now here, we typically start by running a plan command whenever we write or modify a configuration file. The plan command compares your local code against the current state of the infrastructure. If this is the first time you are creating resources, the plan step tells you what will be added. In a scenario where you already have existing resources, the same plan step highlights any differences, such as a new size for an instance or an adjusted attribute on a resource.

The output might look something like:

```
opentofu plan
```

After a brief processing period, OpenTofu shows a summary that includes a list of actions, such as "+ create" for new resources or "~ update" if a resource is changing. If something is being removed, it appears with a "- destroy" notation. If you have multiple files or multiple providers, everything merges into a single plan output, letting you see the overall effect of your changes in one spot.

When you review the plan, you can make sure your code is correct. For example, if you accidentally changed the AMI ID in an EC2 resource and the plan says to replace the instance completely, you will know that the environment might be disrupted. You can decide if that's okay or go back and change the AMI ID. With a clear preview, you can tweak the configuration and run the plan again until the outcome matches what you actually want.

Executing Apply Step

When you are satisfied with the plan, you move forward by running:

```
opentofu apply
```

You might see a prompt asking for confirmation. If you say yes, OpenTofu can take action based on the plan's analysis. It'll create or update resources in real time and communicate with the designated provider or providers. If you are adding a new instance, you will see a short log of the creation process. For a bucket, it'll quickly appear in the right cloud console. But if the environment is big, the apply step might take a while while waiting for certain tasks—like provisioning a database or configuring a load balancer—to finish.

After apply finishes, OpenTofu updates the local state file (or remote state if configured). This file reflects the new reality, linking each resource in your code to the actual resource identifiers in the platform. If you rerun a plan immediately after apply, it typically reports zero changes, indicating that everything is now in the desired state.

Observing Workflow in our Book Publishing Project

If the sample publishing application currently declares a single EC2 instance and a bucket, the plan step shows you both items are to be created if they do not yet exist. Suppose you have something like:

```
resource "aws_instance" "my_ec2" {
  ami           = "ami-12345678"
  instance_type = "t2.micro"
}
resource "aws_s3_bucket" "my_bucket" {
  bucket = "my-example-bucket-123"
  acl    = "private"
}
```

After running the plan and confirming the details, you apply and watch as OpenTofu spins up the instance, configures the storage, and logs the final outcome. This process is your feedback loop for each change you make. If you later decide to rename the bucket or change the instance size, you edit these blocks, run the plan, and see a new set of changes. If a resource is set to be replaced or removed, that also appears in the plan summary.

In this manner, the plan command acts like a safety net, and applying solidifies those changes. Over time, if you expand the publishing application to include load balancers, IAM roles, or databases, the same plan-and-apply pattern remains your primary way of rolling out updates.

Summary

So, in this chapter, you got the initial settings all set up, figured out the providers, and hooked everything up to cloud services like AWS. That lets you manage your cloud resources like a pro. You also got your configuration files in order, following best practices that made your projects easier to read and maintain. Then, you used simple OpenTofu scripts to create basic resources like virtual machines, storage accounts, and networking components.

You got to know the whole lifecycle of OpenTofu commands, like initialization, planning, and applying changes. You learned how each step was crucial for smooth deployments and consistent infrastructure updates. You even figured out how to deal with common issues by using troubleshooting techniques, which gave you the skills to debug configurations and resolve errors effectively.

Chapter 3: Exploring OpenTofu for Applications

Introduction

In this new chapter, I'm focusing on how to shape a book publishing application in a consistent manner using OpenTofu. I'd like to define the project's background and the requirements that drive each infrastructure element. The aim is to see how these components fit together, from hosting the core functionality to handling data and network setup. I'm approaching this with a basic blueprint: a web-based system for uploading and managing manuscripts. By mapping each part to the associated resource in OpenTofu, I'm setting the stage for deeper involvement with real-life deployments. Each detail will clarify these building blocks function seamlessly.

In the first topic, I'm outlining the general scope of the publishing environment, focusing on features that provide a clear reason for each resource. I'm identifying the specific tasks involved, such as uploading manuscripts, handling editorial workflows, and distributing final outputs. Alongside these tasks, I'm interpreting how core components, including a web server, a storage system, or a database, might work. Each element has an essential role in the system, so it's practical to see where OpenTofu enters the picture. The idea is that once these pieces are defined, the actual coding of infrastructure feels straightforward and quite easily adaptable.

In the remaining topics, I'm mapping each requirement to OpenTofu resources. For instance, a storage module might handle manuscript uploads, while a compute element processes the data. I'm also shaping a clear directory layout for code files, so each segment can be found without confusion. This structure usually includes separate sections for providers, resource declarations, and environment variables. By the end of this exploration, you will see how distinct tasks fit together and get ready for more specialized configurations in real-time usage.

Core Components of App

Compute Requirements

When it comes to this publishing system, it can use at least one virtual machine, container, or managed platform to handle the main backend tasks. In many cases, a simple instance running an application or web framework is enough for initial stages. This instance could manage user requests, process manuscript files, and coordinate data exchanges with other services. If the workload grows, scaling could involve adding more instances or shifting to a container-based setup. For the moment, though, you can settle on a single compute block to keep things clear. That block will likely reference an image identifier or container specification, plus a sizing parameter that meets your initial resource needs.

Storage Requirements

Here, we see two main needs for storing content in this book publishing system. One is a general data store for user profiles, submissions, and associated metadata. Another might be an object storage service, which could hold the actual manuscripts in PDF, DOCX, or other file formats.

If you rely on AWS, that might translate into a simple S3 bucket for file uploads, plus a database service for structured details. If your environment extends elsewhere, you can adapt to each platform's equivalent. The intent is that the application can retrieve, update, and store data securely.

Networking Requirements

We also see a need to define a network that allows secure access to the application's core components. That might involve subnets, security group configurations, and possibly route tables if it sits inside a cloud-based VPC setup. The primary goal is to allow users to upload manuscripts while ensuring that the core systems remain restricted from unnecessary external traffic. One or more ports might open for HTTP or HTTPS traffic, giving a straightforward interface to the end users. In some situations, an internal private subnet holds the database, while the compute instance resides in a public or DMZ-like subnet. That arrangement keeps sensitive data less exposed.

Mapping Infrastructure to OpenTofu

Structuring Modules and Resources

We can now define modules for repeated patterns, such as spinning up compute instances with similar characteristics or creating storage buckets for different environments. Each module may have a small set of variables—like region, naming conventions, or capacity settings—that you can tweak between development and production. A resource might represent the actual instance, while a related resource block handles its associated network rules. By linking them, you keep the code self-documented and reduce guesswork about interdependencies. This helps you add, remove, or update entire stacks of functionality without rewriting everything from scratch.

Connecting Components

We can also think of having a module named "compute_module" that accepts arguments such as image ID or instance type, and a "storage_module" for managing object stores or databases. When you integrate both in the main configuration, you see that the compute side references the storage service for read or write operations. Network definitions may sit in their own module as well, controlling subnets, security groups, or private links. By keeping each block dedicated to a distinct function, you preserve the flexibility to shift or reuse them in another environment. For example, staging and production might share the same modules but differ in some variable values, like instance size or storage retention settings. My root configuration file orchestrates how these modules fit together.

Summing Up

Once we have set the basic modules, you declare them in a main `.tf` file, specifying references like:

```
module "compute_part" {
  source      = "./modules/compute_module"
  instance_id = "my_initial_instance"
  # Other variables
}
module "storage_part" {
  source    = "./modules/storage_module"
  bucket_id = "my-manuscripts-bucket"
  # More variables
}
```

When you run plan and then apply, you will see how each module spins up the resources you have linked to your provider. Every time you add a new component—like a database—you can create a new module or expand an existing one. That structure grows with the project, supporting additional features that might arise as the publishing system becomes more complex.

Organizing Codebase

A well-structured project helps you keep track of various files, references, and modules as the application evolves. Now, up to this point, you have written provider blocks in one file, resource definitions in another, and possibly tested a small module or two. That approach is fine for a small pilot, but as soon as you introduce more resources—like load balancers, databases, or multiple S3 buckets—things can become tangled if everything sits in a single directory without a clear naming convention. One way to handle this is by creating dedicated folders for providers, modules, and any environment-specific overrides. For instance, you might keep a root folder called **book-publishing-app** that holds subfolders named **modules**, **environments**, and **providers**. If you keep placing environment-specific files under an **environments/dev** or **environments/prod** subfolder, it ensures that each workspace or environment remains distinct, while still referencing the same shared modules. That layer of organization clarifies exactly where to locate or modify code when adding new services, changing instance types, or adjusting environment variables.

And, inside **modules**, you can group resource definitions by function. For example, a **compute_module** folder might contain files that declare an EC2 instance with optional networking resources, while a **storage_module** folder handles S3 buckets or database definitions. Each module might expose input variables that let you pass in instance sizes, bucket names, or region settings from the root configuration. If your project eventually needs more specialized modules, such as a logging module or a distribution module for static content, you can create fresh subfolders that keep everything consistent. A few lines in a primary **.tf** file in your root directory can then call those modules, passing in the necessary parameters. When you apply the configuration, OpenTofu locates each module and builds the infrastructure in a predictable pattern.

To reflect the earlier steps, you can place the core provider file—perhaps **provider.tf**—in a top-level folder or a dedicated **providers** folder, referencing it across multiple configurations. That file can keep things clean by defining your AWS provider, along with any region or alias preferences. Meanwhile, the root configuration might hold environment-agnostic variables or an overarching main file that orchestrates the modules. Each environment-specific folder could then store variable files and a small **.tf** to point to the correct modules with environment-centric values. If you want to replicate the project for staging, production, or even a special test environment, you simply duplicate the relevant environment folder and tweak the variables. This setup preserves clarity, so that you do not risk mixing up development configurations with those for production.

Summary

We know that this chapter looked at the whole scope of a book publishing environment. It started with a clear look at the project's computing, storage, and networking requirements. You saw how a dedicated instance or container could process submissions, how object storage or a database could handle manuscript files, and how subnets or security rules would ensure secure interactions. Each part of the application showed a practical way to build a system that authors and editors could use without having to do a bunch of manual steps.

Then, we explored the idea of using this infrastructure to create well-organized code. You saw how modules could group related resources—like a compute module for virtual machines and a storage module for buckets and databases—making the whole setup more streamlined. You also saw that a consistent folder structure would help reduce confusion as the application grew in complexity, so that each environment or component lived in its rightful place. The idea of reusing the same modules across different stages or accounts showed how easily things could scale. After looking at all these aspects, you had a clear path to building, maintaining, and evolving a publishing platform that provides an upload process, data storage, and network handling under a unified IaC methodology.

CHAPTER 4: ADVANCED RESOURCE MANAGEMENT

Introduction

We will now be focusing on deeper aspects of managing resources declared in our earlier configurations. You begin by looking at how to handle dependencies among them, ensuring that each resource appears in the correct order so there are no surprises when OpenTofu attempts creation or updates. This ordering can be crucial if one element of the infrastructure must be fully available before another is introduced. You will see that the plan command can help clarify these relationships, and you can reference resources accordingly so that the deployment flow remains orderly.

We will also explore how to update resources once they have been placed, along with the process for removing them gracefully if they are no longer required. It is helpful to know that changing an attribute might result in a new instance or a simple in-place modification, and you can control that behavior by reviewing the plan output. Destroying resources, on the other hand, will be managed with caution, because you do not want to risk deleting important data or leaving partial configurations behind. Lastly, you will take a look at customizing resource attributes to tailor them to the application's evolving needs, whether that involves network ports, advanced parameter tweaks, or adding extra metadata. All of these details prepare you to handle more advanced infrastructure tasks using a code-driven model.

Managing Resource Dependencies

Demonstrating Dependencies with a Publishing Application

Let us consider that our application needs a dedicated bucket for storing manuscripts before a server instance begins processing them. One approach uses references so that the instance looks at attributes from the bucket, which prompts OpenTofu to arrange creation accordingly.

Below is a quick program that shows how one can connect an S3 bucket to an instance through a policy and an IAM role, ensuring the instance deploys only after the policy is ready:

```
# S3 bucket for manuscripts
resource "aws_s3_bucket" "manuscript_store" {
  bucket = "my-book-manuscripts-123"
}
# Simple IAM policy referencing that bucket
resource "aws_iam_policy" "upload_policy" {
  name = "upload-policy"
  path = "/"
```

```
  policy = <<EOF
{
  "Version": "2012-10-17",
  "Statement": [
    {
      "Action": [
        "s3:PutObject",
        "s3:GetObject"
      ],
      "Effect": "Allow",
      "Resource": "arn:aws:s3:::my-book-manuscripts-123/*"
    }
  ]
}
EOF
}
# IAM role (assume it's declared in the same or another file)
resource "aws_iam_role" "upload_role" {
  name = "upload-role"
  assume_role_policy =
data.aws_iam_policy_document.ec2_trust.json
}
# Attach the upload policy to the role
resource "aws_iam_role_policy_attachment" "upload_role_attach"
{
  role       = aws_iam_role.upload_role.name
  policy_arn = aws_iam_policy.upload_policy.arn
}
# Instance profile that references the role
resource "aws_iam_instance_profile" "upload_profile" {
```

```
  name = "upload-instance-profile"
  roles = [aws_iam_role.upload_role.name]
}
# EC2 instance that depends on the policy (and effectively on the bucket through it)
resource "aws_instance" "manuscript_processor" {
  ami           = "ami-12345678"
  instance_type = "t2.micro"
  # This line enforces that the instance only starts once the policy is set
  depends_on = [
    aws_iam_role_policy_attachment.upload_role_attach
  ]
  iam_instance_profile = aws_iam_instance_profile.upload_profile.name
  tags = {
    Name = "ManuscriptProcessor"
  }
}
```

In the above example, the S3 bucket is created first. The IAM policy references that bucket name in its JSON statement, which means OpenTofu automatically recognizes an internal dependency on the bucket's existence. The policy is attached to the role, which leads to the instance profile referencing the role. By including the **depends_on** parameter in the instance, the plan step knows not to deploy the instance until the policy attachment is finalized. If you omit that manual dependency reference, OpenTofu might still infer some of it from referencing resource attributes, but a direct **depends_on** ensures full clarity.

Chaining Dependencies through Outputs

If you later decide to store the bucket name in a module output, and the instance references that module output, OpenTofu automatically deduces that the module must be processed first. For example, a module named "manuscript_storage_module" could export the final bucket name via an output block. Then the EC2 resource that requires that bucket name will read something like **bucket = module.manuscript_storage_module.bucket_name**. During the plan step, the system sees the relationship and positions the manuscript_storage_module resources before the instance. If you define a load balancer that must register the instance as a target, referencing that instance ID in the load balancer config prompts OpenTofu to build the instance first. By letting references do the heavy lifting, you avoid writing multiple **depends_on** lines, unless you have a more implicit dependency that the system cannot detect.

Avoiding Timing Conflicts

When building more advanced features, such as a database resource that the instance queries at startup, referencing an attribute like **db_instance_endpoint = aws_db_instance.author_metadata.endpoint** means the instance block depends on the database's readiness. If the database changes, the plan might indicate that the instance must reconfigure its environment variables or be replaced. This helps keep everything in sync automatically. One does not have to guess the order; the plan step draws from references to create a dependency map, preventing partial builds that would fail.

If you need extra control, the **depends_on** parameter steps in. For example, if the instance must wait for a manual script to finish that the code does not reference directly, you add a resource representing that script or local exec provisioner, then list it in depends_on. The moment the plan processes that line, it sequences the tasks. Once that resource has been executed, only then does the instance proceed. By combining references and, when necessary, explicitly depends_on instructions, you guarantee a stable deployment order. That technique proves especially important in a multi-service architecture, like a publishing system that might have queue services, container tasks, or domain DNS records.

Through references in resource blocks and occasional depends_on usage, you maintain a fully orchestrated flow for the publishing application. When you run plan, you get a graph of how everything interlinks. The moment you type apply, each piece rolls out in sequence. That structure can be expanded to include more microservices or data pipelines. No matter how big the environment gets, if you point it to the right resources, it'll know exactly what steps to take first. This makes sure your deployment is reliable and consistent every time.

Resource Updates and Changes

A need often arises to adjust resources declared in the code, possibly because requirements for the application changed or the infrastructure must scale up. One might switch from a small EC2 instance to a larger type, or alter the bucket properties to enable versioning. Whatever the case, OpenTofu's plan step reveals whether a resource can be updated in place or must be replaced entirely. For instance, changing tags or minor attributes like user data usually prompts an in-place update. By contrast, certain fields (such as an AMI) can trigger a destroy-and-recreate sequence. If the plan indicates a resource will be replaced, that might involve downtime or data loss unless a backup strategy is in place, though specifics vary by resource type.

Following is a quick program that helps to illustrate this point:

```
resource "aws_instance" "manuscript_processor" {
  ami           = "ami-12345678"
  instance_type = "t2.micro"
  tags = {
    Name = "Processor1"
  }
}
```

If you need more compute power for the instance, you can update the instance type:

```
resource "aws_instance" "manuscript_processor" {
  ami           = "ami-12345678"
  instance_type = "t2.medium"
  tags = {
    Name = "Processor1"
  }
}
```

At this point, running **opentofu plan** reveals whether it will replace or merely change attributes. For an AWS instance, changing the instance type might require a new resource creation because it is often not an in-place property. If plan shows a line like **-/+ aws_instance.manuscript_processor**, it signals that the old one will be destroyed and a new one created. If the same code is used for a resource that supports in-place updates, plan might show a **~** symbol to denote an in-place modification. You check the output carefully to confirm what will happen. If it is a replace action, the instance might be replaced, which can drop any data on that particular VM unless you handle it externally or store it on a separate volume.

Other changes involve toggling an attribute like enabling versioning on an S3 bucket. If you initially wrote:

```
resource "aws_s3_bucket" "manuscript_archive" {
  bucket = "my-book-manuscripts-archive-123"
  acl    = "private"
}
```

and decide that versioning is necessary for revision tracking:

```
resource "aws_s3_bucket_versioning" "bucket_versioning" {
  bucket = aws_s3_bucket.manuscript_archive.id
  versioning_configuration {
    status = "Enabled"
  }
}
```

This addition introduces a new resource that references the existing bucket, so plan notes that it must create that resource. The bucket resource itself might remain untouched, but the environment will gain that new versioning configuration object. Here, no replacement of the bucket occurs, unless you also change something within the bucket resource that triggers a forced re-creation. If the plan step shows no replacement on the bucket, applying the changes updates the existing environment. Then the state file indicates that versioning is now associated with that bucket. If at a later point you disable versioning, you might set **`status = "Suspended"`**, and plan would reveal whether it can just adjust the existing versioning configuration.

Sometimes, the environment includes references that cause a chain reaction. For example, if the instance references a network interface declared elsewhere, changing a property of that interface could lead to the instance block reconfiguring. Perhaps you switch the subnet or security group. If plan shows a resource replacement, you can double-check the references. Suppose you rename a subnet resource from "**`aws_subnet.main_subnet`**" to "**`aws_subnet.primary_subnet`**". The instance block that references "**`aws_subnet.main_subnet.id`**" would prompt a mismatch if you do not update it to "**`aws_subnet.primary_subnet.id`**." That leads to plan interpreting it as the old subnet disappearing, the new one appearing, and thus the instance requiring a fresh assignment.

If a big change is truly necessary, like swapping a resource with a brand-new module or shifting from single-instance to a cluster-based approach, you first define the new resources in the code. Then you plan to see how many additions and deletions the system expects. If the environment is large, that process might appear in a more extensive plan output. Once everything is ready, you confirm by applying. This cycle keeps the code as the single source of truth, and when the changes are complete, the state file is updated to reflect the new reality. If the system is not yet correct, or the plan includes unexpected replacements, you revert or fix the code and run the plan again.

Another scenario emerges if you rename a resource block label. For example, changing "**`aws_instance.manuscript_processor`**" to "**`aws_instance.processor_ec2`**" can lead to a plan output that shows a destroyed resource and a created resource. That label is how the code references the resource in the state. If you do not want the resource to be replaced, you can import the old one to the new label or use the state manipulation commands to rename references inside the state. That approach is more advanced but avoids downtime. Without importing or adjusting the state, the code sees the old label as removed and the new label as something brand new. This can be acceptable in a development environment but might disrupt a production system.

In the publishing application, another angle might be altering the IAM roles assigned to the instance. If you initially gave it a role that allowed read/write access to a bucket, then realized you need to add database read permissions, you can expand the IAM policy or attach a second policy to the role. The plan step might show an in-place update of the role if the resource supports partial modifications. If it does not, it might show a replacement of the role resource, prompting the instance to cycle as well.

Destroying Resources Safely

It might be that you added a server or a database that you no longer need. The first step is usually to take out the resource block from your configuration. That'll show the plan output, and you will see the pending destruction. If a resource was declared like this:

```
resource "aws_instance" "extra_server" {
  ami           = "ami-987654321"
  instance_type = "t2.micro"
  tags = {
    Name = "ExtraServer"
  }
}
```

Now here, removing or commenting it out in the file means the next plan run shows **`- destroy`** for that item. That preview indicates OpenTofu wants to decommission the underlying instance. You can inspect the plan to confirm no unintended dependencies are triggered. If you notice that your main application's environment references this server, you might need to revise or remove that reference first. Without doing so, plan might propose other changes if the resource was crucial to the flow. If that is the case, fix any references to avoid surprises when the resource is removed.

Sometimes you only want to remove a single resource, rather than applying every change in the entire configuration. One approach is to use the **`-target`** parameter when running apply or destroy, focusing on the resource you wish to decommission. For example:

```
opentofu plan -target=aws_instance.extra_server
opentofu apply -target=aws_instance.extra_server
```

That sequence ensures the plan and apply commands only affect the targeted server. This method is particularly helpful if a significant number of unrelated changes are in progress elsewhere in the code. By limiting the scope, you reduce the risk of accidentally modifying or destroying other components in the environment. Once the server is removed, you can finalize any leftover references that might remain in the code, or reorganize your modules if this server was part of a larger pattern.

In a publishing application, unused data stores might also remain in the form of a database or an S3 bucket that is no longer required. If a bucket was created for early testing, removing the relevant block in a `.tf` file prompts the plan output to show it under the "destroy" heading. Before applying, you can decide whether any data inside that bucket needs archiving. If the bucket is truly disposable, proceed with apply. If it contains manuscripts or logs you wish to keep, you might transfer them to another storage location first. Skipping that step could result in losing data. When you apply, the resource is removed from the environment and from the state file, keeping everything aligned. If you had an IAM policy referencing that bucket, the plan might also indicate changes to the policy or removal of policy attachments. Make any needed edits so these references are resolved properly. Once that is done, a new plan shows a consistent environment that no longer includes the unused bucket.

Another scenario involves stepping down from a multi-node setup to a single node, perhaps if the load is lighter than expected. In that case, you might remove or comment out resources for additional EC2 instances, load balancers, or auto-scaling blocks. The plan identifies all those items as candidates for destruction. Examining the plan ensures that the main instance or base environment is not inadvertently slated for removal. If everything looks correct, apply finalizes the removal of the unneeded nodes. Any references to the removed nodes—for example, in the security group or route table—also must be updated or removed to avoid leftover dependencies.

At times, a module might encapsulate the entire resource set you want to decommission. If you decide a particular feature is obsolete, removing that module call from the configuration signals that all resources within the module are no longer needed. A plan shows each resource being destroyed. This is convenient if you previously wrapped a group of resources, such as a specialized file-processing stack, into a dedicated module. It simplifies removing everything related to that feature in one edit. Just be prepared to handle any data or references outside the module. If the module had an output that fed into another module, you might revise those references to prevent errors in the plan step.

If you suspect a resource might still be in partial use, run a plan before removing any code. Review references or outputs in your modules to see whether something else depends on that resource. You could also consider a two-phase approach: first, remove the references in the dependent code, apply that change, and confirm that nothing breaks. Then in a second phase, remove the resource block itself. This minimizes disruptions by ensuring that the environment is not left in a half-broken state if a single application tries to do everything simultaneously. Checking the plan at each step ensures you stay aware of each proposed action.

When you finally apply the removal changes, OpenTofu updates the state file to reflect that the resource no longer exists. The Rerun plan should show no further actions needed, confirming a clean state. If you accidentally deleted code for a resource that still physically exists, you might see drift in the environment if it was created outside of OpenTofu or by a previous version of the code. In that case, the plan might not mention the resource at all, since the code no longer tracks it.

Customizing Resource Attributes

There are situations where the application demands slight or significant attribute tweaks for resources. Suppose the publishing system's EC2 instance now requires extra metadata or a startup script to prepare its environment. You can adjust your existing instance resource block by adding user data or modifying a network interface.

For example:

```
resource "aws_instance" "manuscript_processor" {
  ami           = "ami-12345678"
  instance_type = "t2.micro"

  # Adding a user data script that configures the server on
startup
  user_data = file("scripts/setup.sh")
  tags = {
    Name = "ManuscriptProcessor"
  }
}
```

When you run a plan next time, OpenTofu notes that the instance's user data has changed. Depending on how the provider implements those attributes, it might apply them in place, or it might require a resource replacement. Reviewing the plan output clarifies whether it's a destroy-and-recreate operation or a simple update to the current instance. If you prefer to avoid destroying the instance but the provider insists on a fresh resource to accommodate new user data, you can decide if it's acceptable or if you need an alternate strategy.

If the application needs stronger restrictions on who can access an S3 bucket, you might add a bucket policy that references an IAM role. Considering we having an **aws_s3_bucket** block already, and you attach a policy like:

```
resource "aws_s3_bucket_policy" "manuscript_policy" {
```

```
  bucket = aws_s3_bucket.manuscript_store.id
  policy = data.aws_iam_policy_document.manuscript_policy.json
}
data "aws_iam_policy_document" "manuscript_policy" {
  statement {
    effect = "Allow"
    actions = [
      "s3:GetObject",
      "s3:PutObject"
    ]
    resources = [
      "${aws_s3_bucket.manuscript_store.arn}/*"
    ]
    principals {
      type        = "AWS"
      identifiers = [aws_iam_role.upload_role.arn]
    }
  }
}
```

We run plan, and it shows a new resource to be created for the bucket policy. If the bucket definition changes (e.g. renaming the bucket or adding versioning), the plan might also show additional modifications. That clarity helps you confirm that the new policy is the only difference. If you see a replacement, it means the new settings force a fresh bucket creation, which might not be desired if the bucket already holds important files. You can then review those attributes to see if a simpler approach exists.

In a different scenario, the application's networking might require customizing the instance's security group rules to open new ports for an additional service. For instance:

```
resource "aws_security_group" "app_sg" {
  name        = "publishing-app-sg"
  vpc_id      = aws_vpc.main.id
```

```
  ingress {
    from_port   = 22
    to_port     = 22
    protocol    = "tcp"
    cidr_blocks = ["10.0.0.0/16"]
  }

  ingress {
    from_port   = 8080
    to_port     = 8080
    protocol    = "tcp"
    cidr_blocks = ["0.0.0.0/0"]
  }

  egress {
    from_port   = 0
    to_port     = 0
    protocol    = "-1"
    cidr_blocks = ["0.0.0.0/0"]
  }
}
```

If the original config only opened port 22 for SSH, and now you have included port 8080 for a new server function, the plan step highlights an in-place update to add that inbound rule. The security group remains the same, but with a changed rule set. If the code references that security group in the instance block, the instance does not typically need to be replaced, as it can accept the new rule dynamically. Observing the plan output confirms that it's a simple modification, preventing disruption to the application.

If the application requires a different AMI to incorporate updated system packages, you can change the AMI ID in the instance resource. For example, switching from **"ami-12345678"** to **"ami-87654321"**. A plan preview might note a destroy-and-recreate action, suggesting that the instance must be rebuilt. This can be acceptable if you have a stateless setup or if you store data externally. If you see a forced replacement in the plan, you schedule that apply for a maintenance window or after copying relevant data. Sometimes, instance type changes can also prompt a replacement. Each attribute has its own rules for whether it can be done in place or not. The plan output remains the best indicator of which route will be taken.

When you add or remove optional parameters, you typically see minor modifications in plan, but occasionally a deeper attribute shift triggers a bigger rebuild. If that's not what you want, you can search for alternate ways to implement the change. For instance, if you only need to run a script once on the instance, you might set up a null_resource with a provisioner referencing the instance, rather than editing user data. If that's acceptable for the publishing workflow, it becomes a small code tweak instead of a major reconfiguration. In either case, the plan step clarifies the consequences.

If the publishing platform begins to rely on a load balancer for better performance, you might declare an **`aws_lb`** resource or an **`aws_alb`** resource, referencing the existing subnets or security groups. That configuration might also require customizing health checks or idle timeouts. When you add these new attributes, the plan typically shows you a create operation for the load balancer, plus any in-place updates for the security group. If you tweak the load balancer further to enable sticky sessions, you see a partial in-place modification or possibly a recreation if that attribute demands a fresh object. For the instance or service behind the load balancer, referencing the load balancer name or ARN enforces the correct order: create the load balancer, then attach the instance or target group. Each step in the code remains under control, with the plan step revealing how large or small the final change is.

Summary

Overall, we realized that dependencies among resources mattered when rolling out new application features. If a server needed a bucket ready before referencing it, you could rely on direct attribute references or the **`depends_on`** parameter to synchronize creation. Whenever a resource needed replacing, such as changing an instance type or adding a user data script, the plan output would reveal whether the action was an in-place update or a full teardown and rebuild. You found it useful to review each plan for those indicators before confirming changes, preventing unnecessary downtime.

We also learned how customizing resource attributes unlocked new possibilities for the publishing environment. We understood that adjusting user data for an instance or adding a bucket policy required only a few code modifications, followed by a plan and then an apply. If a minor adjustment led to a forced replacement, you could evaluate the plan and delay the action to a more convenient time. The same pattern repeated whenever a new security group setting, load balancer, or database tweak appeared. Each attribute change ensured the environment could grow without losing alignment between the code and real resources.

Chapter 5: Reusability with OpenTofu Modules

Introduction

In this chapter, we are shifting our focus to creating modules that bundle related resources, which can simplify and speed up deployments. Now, each piece of a module might include a main file for the resource definitions, a variables file to parameterize the configuration, and an output file that shares results with the rest of the setup. These variables can handle things like instance sizing or naming specifics, so you can give different values for dev, staging, or prod without rewriting resource blocks. Modules can also produce outputs that pass info back to the parent configuration, like the ID of a newly created server or the URL of a storage bucket.

The final part teaches about how to keep module code in a version-controlled environment. This way, you can avoid accidentally overwriting something, and it'll keep a record of each change in a repository. When a module is improved or patched, referencing a specific version or commit in multiple configurations keeps everything consistent. And if more advanced changes are needed later on, you can just bump the version of that module and test it in a safe environment. By keeping track of reusable modules in a system, you can grow your infrastructure without too much chaos, even as new requirements pop up.

Creating Your First Module

Here, we can start with setting up a folder named **modules** in your project directory. Inside that folder, you create a subfolder for a simple resource grouping—perhaps a container for an EC2 instance and its supporting components. The name of this subfolder could be something like **compute_module**. Within that subfolder, you place three primary files: **main.tf**, **variables.tf**, and **outputs.tf**. The idea is that **main.tf** holds the resource blocks, **variables.tf** lists any adjustable parameters you want to expose, and **outputs.tf** provides references that a calling configuration can retrieve.

A typical **variables.tf** file might look like:

```
variable "instance_type" {
  type    = string
  default = "t2.micro"
}
variable "ami_id" {
  type    = string
}
variable "instance_name" {
```

```
  type    = string
  default = "DefaultInstance"
}
```

In the above example, you accept three variables: one for the instance type, one for the AMI, and one for a name tag. No specialized logic is needed—just a straightforward definition of parameters. You could add more if the module must handle networking or security. Each variable can have an optional default, letting you skip specifying it if you are satisfied with the default value.

In **main.tf**, you place the resource blocks. Let's say you want to create an EC2 instance in AWS:

```
resource "aws_instance" "module_ec2" {
  ami           = var.ami_id
  instance_type = var.instance_type
  tags = {
    Name = var.instance_name
  }
}
```

By referencing **var.instance_type**, **var.ami_id**, and **var.instance_name**, you link the resource to the variables defined in **variables.tf**. If the environment references an AWS provider, it can find these resources automatically, provided that the root configuration or the calling module includes that provider. Some choose to define a local provider block here, but often one can rely on the root configuration to specify providers for all modules to use, especially if multiple modules share the same provider setup.

In **outputs.tf**, you store any values that might be helpful to the parent configuration. For example:

```
output "instance_id" {
  description = "The ID of the EC2 instance"
  value       = aws_instance.module_ec2.id
}
output "public_ip" {
  description = "The public IP address of the instance"
  value       = aws_instance.module_ec2.public_ip
```

```
}
```

That way, after the module completes creation, you can retrieve **mo,ule.compute_module.instance_id** or **module.compute_module.public_ip** in the calling configuration. These details might prove valuable for referencing other resources, such as a load balancer or a DNS record.

We then move back to the root of your project or an environment-specific folder, where you include a block that invokes this new module. For example, in a file named **main.tf**:

```
module "compute_module" {
  source          = "./modules/compute_module"
  ami_id          = "ami-12345678"
  instance_type   = "t2.micro"
  instance_name   = "PublishingCompute"
}
```

When you run **opentofu init**, it sees the local module path and prepares everything. The plan command compares the module's resource definitions plus the provided variables to see what changes it should create or update. You might see that the module is creating an EC2 instance named "PublishingCompute" with an AMI "ami-12345678." If you decide you want a different instance size, you only change **instance_type** in the module block, run plan again, and see if a replacement or in-place update occurs.

If your publishing application requires multiple instances with different roles, you can call the same module multiple times with varied parameters. For instance:

```
module "compute_module_backend" {
  source          = "./modules/compute_module"
  ami_id          = "ami-11111111"
  instance_type   = "t2.small"
  instance_name   = "BackendProcessor"
}
module "compute_module_frontend" {
  source          = "./modules/compute_module"
  ami_id          = "ami-22222222"
  instance_type   = "t2.small"
```

```
  instance_name   = "FrontendDisplay"
}
```

That way, you re-use the same logic while passing unique AMI IDs or naming conventions. Each block is recognized as a separate instance of the module, producing its own set of resources, which appear in the plan output. If the module includes outputs like "public_ip," each call has a distinct value. So if you need the backend's IP address in some other resource, you can reference module.compute_module_backend.public_ip.

With the publishing application in mind, the module might incorporate references to an IAM role that grants permission to an S3 bucket for manuscript uploads. If that bucket name or ARN is also parameterized, you can feed it in from the parent configuration. For instance, a variable named **manuscript_bucket_arn** might let the module attach a role policy referencing that bucket. The root module, or a separate resource definition, may create the actual bucket, then pass its ARN. This method ensures you keep the compute logic (EC2 resources, roles, user data) in one place, and the storage logic (S3 bucket, versioning, etc.) in another. If you choose to store the S3 creation steps in a separate "storage_module," you might have two modules in your project: one for compute, another for storage. Then your main configuration calls each module. The storage module might output the final bucket ARN, which you feed into the compute module. That fosters a clearer mental map of the environment, matching how the publishing application might be structured in real life.

Input Variables in Modules

We can build a module that launches an EC2 instance and attaches a security group, yet you want the flexibility to choose the instance size, region, or even a custom script for initialization. That's where input variables come into play. Suppose the application uses multiple environments like dev, staging, and production. Each environment might have distinct requirements for compute power or naming conventions. By exposing something like **instance_type**, **environment_name**, or **startup_script** as variables, you can pass different values to the same module.

Let's consider that you have a folder named **modules/compute_unit** where you house a few resources, like an EC2 instance and a security group.

Now here within **variables.tf**, you can define:

```
variable "instance_type" {
  type    = string
  default = "t2.micro"
}
```

```
variable "environment_name" {
  type    = string
  default = "dev"
}
variable "startup_script" {
  type    = string
  default = ""
}
```

The main resource file, **main.tf**, references these variables:

```
resource "aws_security_group" "module_sg" {
  name        = "${var.environment_name}-sg"
  description = "Security group for ${var.environment_name}
environment"
  # Additional rules if needed, omitted here for brevity
}
resource "aws_instance" "module_ec2" {
  ami           = data.aws_ami.ubuntu.id
  instance_type = var.instance_type
  user_data     = var.startup_script
  vpc_security_group_ids = [
    aws_security_group.module_sg.id
  ]
  tags = {
    Name = "${var.environment_name}-ec2"
  }
}
```

A user might keep the lookup for an Ubuntu AMI in a data source, which references a publicly available image in the region that the AWS provider sets. The security group name depends on the environment name, effectively labeling your resources dev-sg or staging-sg. The instance tags also reflect that environment. The **startup_script** variable might hold a file path read through the file function in the parent configuration, so each environment can run a unique set of configuration commands upon boot.

Once you have set up those variables and resources, you move back to your main configuration file (outside the module folder) and call the module with specific arguments:

```
module "my_compute_unit" {
  source           = "./modules/compute_unit"
  instance_type    = "t2.small"
  environment_name = "staging"
  startup_script   = file("scripts/staging_init.sh")
}
```

This above code instructs the module to use a t2.small instance size, label resources with staging in the names, and run a staging-specific script at startup. If you need a production environment that uses a bigger instance type and a different script, you just call the same module block again under a different name, changing those variables:

```
module "my_compute_unit_prod" {
  source           = "./modules/compute_unit"
  instance_type    = "t3.medium"
  environment_name = "production"
  startup_script   = file("scripts/prod_init.sh")
}
```

Each call results in a unique set of resources: one environment referencing t2.small, another referencing t3.medium, all derived from the same module code. By running plan, you can see the separate resources that will appear for each environment. The security group names differ, the instance tags differ, and the startup scripts differ, but the code structure in **main.tf** inside the module remains the same.

Input variables can also be used to toggle optional features in a module. For instance, you might have a boolean variable named **enable_public_ip** in the module's variables. If it's set to true, you set **associate_public_ip_address = true** in the instance block; if false, you skip it. This pattern gives you an on/off switch for a public IP, which could be environment-specific.

Consider the following example:

```
resource "aws_instance" "module_ec2" {
  ami           = data.aws_ami.ubuntu.id
  instance_type = var.instance_type
  associate_public_ip_address = var.enable_public_ip ? true :
false
  # ...
}
```

When dev sets **enable_public_ip = false**, the plan shows the instance lacking a public IP, whereas production might set that variable to true, prompting the instance to allocate a public IP. Everything else in the code is identical, but the variable drives the difference in outcome. You can expand that logic further if you want to conditionally create or skip entire resources, though that typically involves more advanced expressions or additional resources that are toggled on or off based on a variable's value. This scales well: a single module might handle a variety of configurations for different use cases, each driven by the input variables passed in from the caller.

If your publishing application needs to evolve further, you can add more variables. For instance, you might define a variable for enabling or disabling a specialized IAM role that grants access to an S3 bucket. The module checks whether that variable is true, then creates the role and attaches a policy referencing the bucket. If it's false, the role block is not used. That pattern helps you avoid rewriting code for separate modules that do almost the same thing. Instead, you keep one flexible module.

When you make changes to the module's **variables.tf** file—like adding a new variable or changing defaults—the plan command in the root configuration can highlight if anything is missing or if the usage in the parent configuration is still valid. If you remove a variable that the parent references, plan might fail because it cannot find that variable in the module anymore. Reviewing the plan output or error messages clarifies how you should adjust the parent configuration. This interplay ensures that any changes remain transparent, and you can fix them quickly.

Input variables effectively serve as parameters that shape each resource in the module. By controlling them, you can deploy highly customized copies of the same resource set across dev, staging, production, or even specialized test environments. As the project grows, you can refine or add more variables to handle new scenarios. If you need a bigger suite of attributes—like subnets, availability zones, or advanced network settings, we just place additional variables in **variables.tf** and reference them within the resources.

This method of passing variables to modules, testing with plan, and applying the changes fosters an environment where each environment is described consistently. If you see that the production environment must run on a different instance type or must attach a second security group, you only tweak the module call in the production block. If a different environment does not require that second security group, the variable controlling it is left at a default or is set to an empty value. The plan step outlines how that difference manifests in the final set of resources. With each iteration, the entire system remains code-based, traceable in version control, and consistently synchronized with actual infrastructure, all thanks to the flexible nature of input variables.

Outputs and Inter-Module Communication

We can continue to build upon the concept of input variables by also defining outputs in a module. These outputs allow a module to pass valuable information back to the configuration that calls it. For instance, if you have a module that creates an EC2 instance, it might expose the instance ID or public IP as outputs, enabling other parts of the configuration to reference these details without writing complex logic. To demonstrate this, you return to the previous module idea for a compute resource and expand it. Suppose you have a **main.tf** that declares the instance and a security group. In addition to the variables file, you introduce an **outputs.tf** file inside the same module folder.

A simple version of **outputs.tf** could be:

```
output "instance_id" {
  description = "The ID of the EC2 instance created by this module"
  value       = aws_instance.module_ec2.id
}
output "security_group_id" {
  description = "The ID of the security group attached to the instance"
  value       = aws_security_group.module_sg.id
}
```

Once these outputs are declared, any configuration that calls the module can reference them by writing something like **module.my_compute_unit.instance_id** or **module.my_compute_unit.security_group_id**. If you decide to spin up another resource that needs the instance ID, you might feed that output into its configuration. For example, a load balancer resource may require a target registration referencing the instance ID. By reading the module's output, the load balancer resource can automatically connect to the correct instance.

Interconnecting Two Modules

If you have a "storage_module" that creates an S3 bucket, you might define an output for the bucket name or ARN in its **outputs.tf**:

```
output "bucket_name" {
  description = "The name of the S3 bucket"
  value       = aws_s3_bucket.manuscript_store.id
}
```

Then in your root configuration, you call the storage module:

```
module "storage_module" {
  source = "./modules/storage_module"
  # Possibly some variables, if needed
}
```

If you want the compute module to have access to that bucket, you can either pass the output from one module directly into another or store it in a local variable first. One way to pass it directly looks like:

```
module "compute_module_backend" {
  source = "./modules/compute_unit"
  # other variables...
  # pass the bucket name if the compute module uses it
  environment_name = "backend"
  # Suppose we have a variable in the compute module for
referencing bucket_name
  bucket_name = module.storage_module.bucket_name
}
```

This links the output **bucket_name** from the storage module to the **bucket_name** variable in the compute module. If the compute module references **var.bucket_name** within its resources—perhaps in an IAM policy or user data script—it can do so seamlessly. During a plan, OpenTofu automatically detects that the storage module must be processed first to output the correct bucket name, which is then passed to the compute module.

Sample Program

Let's take a small scenario, wherein the compute module needs an IAM policy that allows reading or writing to the S3 bucket produced by the storage module. That might look like this in **`main.tf`** inside the compute module:

```
variable "bucket_name" {
  type = string
}
resource "aws_iam_policy" "allow_bucket_access" {
  name   = "${var.environment_name}-bucket-access"
  path   = "/"
  policy = data.aws_iam_policy_document.bucket_access.json
}
data "aws_iam_policy_document" "bucket_access" {
  statement {
    effect = "Allow"
    actions = [
      "s3:GetObject",
      "s3:PutObject"
    ]
    resources = [
      "arn:aws:s3:::${var.bucket_name}/*"
    ]
  }
}
```

Since **`var.bucket_name`** references the storage module's output in the root configuration, the plan step sees that the storage module must generate the actual bucket first, returning the name. Only then can the compute module create an IAM policy pointing to that name. This chain ensures consistent ordering, so there's no confusion about which resource is created first. If you rename the bucket in the storage module, the plan step picks that up, adjusts the policy, and might apply an in-place update or a replacement, depending on how the policy handles changes.

Reading Outputs in other Resources

You can also reference one module's outputs inside another module's inputs and attach those outputs to resources in the same root configuration. For example, if you make a DNS record that points to the compute module's public IP, you can do something like:

```
resource "aws_route53_record" "backend_dns" {
  zone_id = "Z1D633PJN98FT9"
  name    = "backend.mydomain.com"
  type    = "A"
  ttl     = 300
  records = [
    module.compute_module_backend.public_ip
  ]
}
```

Here, **public_ip** is presumably an output from the compute module that references **aws_instance.module_ec2.public_ip**. If you rename the instance or switch the instance to a new region, the output changes. The next plan reflects that new IP, and the **aws_route53_record** resource updates automatically. That saves you from hardcoding IP addresses or juggling them manually in multiple places.

Testing and Verifying

Now, when you run **opentofu plan**, you see how resources from multiple modules fit together. If a new or changed output is introduced in the storage module, and you haven't updated the compute module's variable references accordingly, the plan or init steps might produce errors indicating the mismatch. Addressing those mismatches typically involves adjusting the variable names or references in each module or the root configuration. This direct feedback loop means you stay aware of how changes in one module ripple through the rest of the setup.

If you decide to rename an output in a module—for example, changing **bucket_name** to **bucket_id**—the plan might fail in places that expect **module.storage_module.bucket_name**. You adapt the calling configuration to reference **module.storage_module.bucket_id**, then re-run plan. That ensures everything is consistent.

Version Control for Modules

A team might store modules in a local folder within the same repository as the main configurations, or they might choose an entirely separate repository for modules that multiple projects can reference. Whichever route is chosen, the key is to keep track of changes so that any adjustments in a module are visible and reversible. If the modules live in a folder named **modules** alongside the root configuration, each edit automatically shows up in version control when the entire project is committed. That single repository approach is often convenient, as the main code and modules evolve together. Once you push changes to a branch, teammates can review how a new feature or fix in the module might affect the root configuration.

Another method involves placing modules in their own repository so multiple projects can reuse them. In that setup, you might reference a Git URL in the **module** block's source field, such as:

```
module "compute_module" {
  source = "git::https://github.com/YourOrg/infra-
modules.git//compute_module?ref=v1.2.0"
  # module variables...
}
```

The suffix **//compute_module** directs OpenTofu to the subfolder within that repository, and the **?ref=v1.2.0** indicates a specific tag or branch. One advantage of this scheme is that you can label each release in the module repository with semantic versions, such as **v1.2.0**. The root configuration pins to that version, providing a predictable state. If a new module version is released, you can test it locally by updating the reference to **?ref=v1.3.0** or a newer tag, then running a plan to see if anything breaks. This gating step keeps you in control of when to adopt changes, rather than letting them slip in unnoticed.

If the team modifies the module repository to fix an issue or add a new feature, they push a commit or tag. At that moment, the main project's plan command doesn't change, because it's still locked to the older reference. Only when you manually bump that **ref** to the updated commit or tag does the root configuration adopt the modifications. This method grants each environment or project the freedom to remain on a stable version while others experiment with the latest module changes. If you decide to manage modules entirely in a private Git repository, an authentication mechanism might be needed so OpenTofu can clone it. That setup typically involves SSH keys or tokens. After configuring the credentials, referencing the module source remains similar, just pointing to the private repository. The process for version locking with **?ref=tag-or-branch** is the same. If the repository is self-hosted, the URL might look like **git@your.internal.repo:team/infra-modules.git**, again specifying the subfolder with **//compute_module**. By pinning to a specific commit hash, you become even more precise, ensuring that no matter how tags shift around, your project always references the exact code. If that commit changes, you will see a different hash in the source line, and the plan clarifies any resulting changes.

If you store modules in a public registry or a private registry, the source line might use a slightly different format. For instance, the Terraform Registry style (which OpenTofu may support similarly) might look like **registry.gitforgits.com/team/compute_module**. That style allows version constraints like **version = "~> 1.2.0"** in a **required_providers** or module block, indicating that anything from 1.2.x is acceptable, but not 1.3.0 or higher. If you rely on the open-source versions of these registries, you can mirror that approach with your own hosting. This general concept remains consistent: you specify a version or version range, and the system fetches the code matching that constraint whenever you run **opentofu init**. If a newer version is published that breaks compatibility, your pinned version ensures no unexpected changes occur until you explicitly decide to move up.

When a module evolves significantly—maybe by adding new variables or renaming outputs—the plan might break if the root configuration references the old names. By versioning each release, you can update the module code incrementally. Suppose you add a new variable named **db_endpoint** or rename **instance_id** to **server_id**. If you push that to a new tag, any root configuration that upgrades must adapt references accordingly. That means you can keep older environments functioning by leaving them at the previous tag, letting them avoid the rename until you are ready to unify everything. This incremental method also aids in code reviews, because you see exactly how one version differs from another. Each tag or commit contains a set of changes that can be reviewed or rolled back if needed.

At times, you might want to patch a module that's pinned in production while continuing other feature development on a main branch. This scenario often leads to release branches or patch branches. You can fix a bug on the **release-1.2** branch, tag it as **v1.2.1**, and then update your production environment from **v1.2.0** to **v1.2.1** without merging in the new feature changes that live on the main branch. Additionally, referencing tags or branches in your root **.tf** files typically happens in a **module** block's **source** parameter if you have placed the code in a remote repository.

Consider the below quick example:

```
module "some_module" {
  source = "git::ssh://git@github.com/YourOrg/infra-
modules.git//some_module?ref=v1.2.1"
  # Pass any required variables here
}
```

If you store everything in a single monolithic repository, you don't need the Git ref mechanism as much; you might rely on branches within that single repo, or you might keep everything on the main branch and trust your code reviews. In that scenario, the environment references the local path **./modules/some_module**, so as soon as you commit changes, the plan picks them up. The advantage is simpler referencing, but the downside is losing the fine-grained version locking you'd get from separate repos or registry-based references.

To see how this might play out in the publishing application, imagine you have a module for launching a specialized instance that processes manuscripts. You store that module in a separate Git repository so the rest of the team can reuse or refine it for other projects. The publishing project references a specific version, say **`v1.0.3`**, which includes the basics needed for the system. If the module maintainers add a new variable for advanced logging, you can wait to adopt it. Once they tag **`v1.1.0`**, you try updating your main code to the new version, run a plan, and notice that certain references must be updated. After making those minor code changes in your root configuration, the plan passes, so you apply them. If anything unexpected appears, you could revert to the old version. In that sense, version control for modules ensures stable, traceable updates for the entire environment.

Summary

We learned a lot about how modules can help you transform repetitive resource blocks into portable units that you can reference from multiple places.Once the resources were grouped in a module folder with main, variables, and outputs files, everything became more structured.Each variable let you pass different values for instance sizes, region settings, or other details, turning a single set of declarations into something adaptable for dev, staging, or production. With outputs, modules could share essential data like EC2 instance IDs or S3 bucket names, making for more dynamic interactions. Different modules could pass references to each other, making sure the whole project worked smoothly without manual lookups or guesswork.

We also realized that managing module versions through a local folder or a separate repository made it more reliable when working with others. We also found that pinning the main configuration to a specific Git tag or commit was key to preventing unplanned code changes from messing with stable environments. With that setup, each environment could stay on a stable version while a new version was being tested in dev. Once everything was in sync, you could update production by just changing the version reference, apply changes, and confirm everything was on track. All of this kept you from getting hit with any nasty surprises when someone updated the module code. It also let you branch and patch older releases as needed.

Chapter 6: State Management in OpenTofu

Introduction

In this chapter, we will be looking at the mechanisms that keep infrastructure definitions synchronized with real resources in the upcoming topics. One primary piece is the state file, which records the exact mapping between code declarations and their corresponding items in the platform. By reviewing that file, you can ensure that each resource is tracked accurately, reducing guesswork or potential mismatches.

Next, we will consider the concept of state drift, which appears when manual changes or external modifications happen outside the code. When that occurs, the plan step might detect differences between the declared configuration and the real-world setup. Identifying these mismatches helps you decide whether to align the code with what actually exists, or revert the infrastructure to match the code's intent. This process keeps everything consistent, even as multiple individuals might interact with the environment.

Finally, you will explore strategies for avoiding collisions when multiple users work on the same project. A locking mechanism ensures that only one person or pipeline can modify the state at a time, preventing partial updates or overwrites that could break deployments. This becomes especially relevant in team-based settings where multiple individuals might run plan and apply simultaneously. By properly handling locks, each change remains controlled and traceable.

Understanding State file

How State file track Infrastructure?

A state file is a record that connects the configurations written in your OpenTofu project to the actual infrastructure resources in your environment. Whenever you declare a resource (such as an instance, bucket, or database), OpenTofu assigns it a logical name in your code. Once that resource is created or updated, OpenTofu stores essential data—like IDs and attributes—in the state file. This file becomes the reference point for future plan operations, letting you see which items have changed or need creation or removal.

OpenTofu compares the state file against both the desired configuration in your **`.tf`** files and the reality in your chosen platform. If something in the code doesn't match what is in the state, the plan command highlights the discrepancy. That might reveal brand-new resources, updates to existing ones, or items that no longer appear in the code. By maintaining these details, the state file helps align your local definitions with the infrastructure's actual status. If you modify a resource's size or region, OpenTofu notices the difference and shows whether the action is an in-place change or a destroy-and-recreate event.

Local State Storage

Some projects store state files locally in the same folder as the configuration. When running

opentofu init for the first time and not specifying a backend, a local file (often named **terraform.tfstate**) is generated. If only one person manages a small project, this way of wroking can be enough. Inspecting the local file reveals JSON-like entries that map resource labels to real IDs, so one can verify data as needed.

An example of using local state might be:

```
cd my-publishing-app

opentofu init

opentofu plan

opentofu apply
```

After these commands, the folder includes a **.tfstate** file reflecting all tracked resources. However, working with local storage can lead to conflicts if multiple teammates run plan or apply on different machines. The risk is that one person's local file might be outdated, causing unintentional overwrites.

Remote State Storage

A lot of teams use remote storage for working together or for running automated pipelines that apply changes from a shared location. With a remote backend, there's only one copy of the state file that's authoritative, so you can avoid mismatched updates. A popular choice is an S3 bucket of AWS, but there are other options too. The key point is that every plan or apply fetches and updates the same file, so there's no confusion about which workstation has the latest details.

Below is a short example of a configuration block that specifies an S3 backend in an OpenTofu-compatible style:

```
opentofu {
  backend "s3" {
    bucket = "my-publishing-state"
    key    = "state-files/production.tfstate"
    region = "us-east-1"
  }
}
provider "aws" {
  region = "us-east-1"
}
```

When running **opentofu init**, OpenTofu prompts for permission to configure the remote backend. It might also ask for credentials if they aren't already set as environment variables. After initialization, the state file resides in the S3 bucket rather than your local folder. The **key** parameter indicates the path inside that bucket, while **region** shows where to find it. Each plan or apply operation locks the remote file (assuming the backend supports locking), so that no one else can modify infrastructure at the same moment. Once the action is complete, the lock is released.

Sample Program: Switching from Local to Remote

If a project started with a local state, migrating it to remote storage can happen through commands that pull the local file up to the chosen backend. One might see a process like:

```
# Initial local usage
opentofu init
opentofu apply
# Then edit the configuration to include the s3 backend
opentofu {
  backend "s3" {
    bucket = "my-publishing-state"
    key    = "state-files/production.tfstate"
    region = "us-east-1"
  }
}
# Re-initialize
opentofu init
```

If OpenTofu detects the new backend, it'll offer to migrate the existing state. After you confirm, the local file merges into the remote location. After that, you can plan and apply references to the copy in S3. If you connect to the same configuration later on, any user or pipeline will have access to the updated file, which helps prevent collisions and makes the environment more reliable in multi-user scenarios.

Handling State Drift

Discrepancies between Code and Real Infra

State drift appears when someone modifies resources outside OpenTofu's normal plan-and-apply cycle. That might happen if a colleague quickly changes a security group rule via the AWS console, or if a script updates tags in the background without reflecting those changes in code. The plan command is often the first indicator of drift, because it analyzes what the current state file expects versus the attributes actually found in the platform. If the plan output shows updates that you did not intend—like a changed port, a missing tag, or an altered resource count—there is a sign that drift might be in play. Sometimes it only appears after a resource is used differently than expected, which can cause an out-of-sync environment and lead to confusion or potential downtime.

One way to detect drift explicitly is through a targeted plan. For instance, if you suspect that an S3 bucket policy changed manually, run:

```
opentofu plan -target=aws_s3_bucket_policy.my_bucket_policy
```

That step inspects only that resource, highlighting any differences. If you see lines indicating that a block was removed or altered, it reveals how the real infrastructure no longer matches the code. You can choose whether to accept the modification and update your **.tf** file accordingly, or revert the infrastructure back to what the code declares. Reviewing the plan details clarifies which path is needed.

Changes Reconciliation

Suppose an IAM policy is updated in the AWS console, and your plan step shows a mismatch. If you want to keep that manual change, you can modify the resource block in the code to match the new settings. Then plan again, see if it becomes an in-place update or if any references need adjusting. Alternatively, if that manual change should never have happened, the next apply step reverts the IAM policy to match the code's version. That reversion is automatic, though it might affect services relying on the new policy. You might see a line in the plan explaining that it will replace or restore certain policy statements to align with your **.tf** file.

There is also a scenario where drift can introduce partial references. Imagine you reference a security group ID in multiple places, and someone deletes or renames that security group outside the code. The plan step might complain it cannot find the security group, or it might propose destroying what remains. A solution is to confirm whether that security group is still needed. If yes, re-create or rename it properly in code, possibly with the same ID if you import it. If it is truly unnecessary, remove references in your code so the plan does not keep searching for it.

Sample Program: Bucket Policy Modified outside Code

Let us consider that our publishing application includes a resource block:

```
resource "aws_s3_bucket" "manuscript_bucket" {
```

```
  bucket = "my-book-manuscripts"
}
resource "aws_s3_bucket_policy" "manuscript_policy" {
  bucket = aws_s3_bucket.manuscript_bucket.id
  policy = data.aws_iam_policy_document.manuscript_iam.json
}
data "aws_iam_policy_document" "manuscript_iam" {
  statement {
    effect    = "Allow"
    actions   = ["s3:GetObject", "s3:PutObject"]
    resources = ["${aws_s3_bucket.manuscript_bucket.arn}/*"]
    principals {
      type        = "AWS"
      identifiers =
["arn:aws:iam::123456789012:role/ManuscriptRole"]
    }
  }
}
```

If someone decides to add a new action, say **s3:DeleteObject**, directly in the AWS console, that edit does not appear in your **.tf** file. Running plan might reveal:

```
# aws_s3_bucket_policy.manuscript_policy will be updated in-
place
  ~ policy = … # old policy lines …
                + "s3:DeleteObject"
```

This indicates the real policy has a delete action that the state file does not expect. You can keep that addition by incorporating it into **data.aws_iam_policy _document.manuscript_iam**. Then the drift disappears because the code matches the actual environment. If you decide it was a mistake, applying your unchanged code removes the extra action, restoring the policy to its original form. The final choice depends on the desired application behavior.

Resolving Orphaned Resources

There are some drift scenarios which involve a resource that was removed in the cloud console, but the **.tf** code still references it. The plan step could show a missing resource error or might propose creating it again. For instance, if an S3 bucket was deleted manually, OpenTofu sees that the state references a bucket ID that no longer exists. A plan step can mention that the resource needs to be recreated. If you wish to keep it gone, remove or comment out the bucket declaration in your **.tf** file and run plan again. That indicates a pending "- destroy" for the resource, but it might not do anything because the item no longer physically exists. After apply, the state file updates so the resource is no longer tracked.

If something is physically present but not in your code, you can import it rather than re-creating or ignoring it. For example:

```
opentofu import aws_instance.existing_server i-0abc123def456
```

That command updates the state to include the instance with the specified ID under the **aws_instance.existing_server** block. Once imported, the plan sees it as part of the normal deployment, preventing confusion. If that resource later changes externally, you revert or adopt those changes just like any other item in your **.tf** files.

Ongoing Maintenance

Sometimes drift gets found through automatic checks or when there are unexpected problems with the infrastructure. If you run a plan a lot in a CI pipeline, it can flag differences early. If something doesn't match up, the build might fail or produce a warning, which will prompt a review. This way, you can be sure that each time you suggest a code change, it's tested against the current environment. If the plan shows unrelated updates, it implies that a manual tweak or drift occurred, and you can handle it before merging new code.

This pattern helps keep the environment stable, letting you focus on the actual changes you want to introduce. They'll probably tell you to avoid manually changing resources in the console. But that might not always work in urgent situations, so drift can still happen. If you review the plan and deal with the issues quickly, you can keep things consistent. If a lot of changes accumulate, like a bunch of resources that weren't updated in the code, it can take some time to get everything back in sync.

State Locking

Why Locking in Multi-User Environments?

Now, imagine a bunch of people are updating the publishing app at the same time. One user might be launching new EC2 instances, while another is adjusting S3 bucket settings. If they both run an apply step at the same time, they'll try to modify the same state file, but with different changes. This can lead to partial updates or even lost information, which can leave the infrastructure in an unpredictable state. But remote state locking solves that problem by enforcing a simple rule: only one plan or apply operation can modify the state file at any given moment. If a second user tries to run apply while the file is locked, the tool notifies them to wait until the lock is released.

Defining Remote State Backend with Locking

A remote backend is typically configured by specifying a provider like AWS S3 or another supported storage service. These services often include locking features—S3 can work with DynamoDB for locks, for example.

Given below is a sample block that might look like:

```
opentofu {
  backend "s3" {
    bucket         = "my-publishing-app-state"
    key            = "environments/prod/state.tfstate"
    region         = "us-east-1"
    # For state locking, specify a DynamoDB table
    dynamodb_table = "publishing-state-lock"
  }
}
provider "aws" {
  region = "us-east-1"
}
```

Now here, when you run **opentofu init**, it automatically checks whether the specified S3 bucket and DynamoDB table exist. If the table does not exist, you might create it manually or through a small resource block:

```
resource "aws_dynamodb_table" "state_lock" {
  name         = "publishing-state-lock"
  billing_mode = "PAY_PER_REQUEST"
  hash_key     = "LockID"
  attribute {
```

```
    name = "LockID"
    type = "S"
  }
}
```

Once that table is in place, each time you run plan or apply, OpenTofu attempts to acquire a lock by writing a record into the DynamoDB table. If a lock is already in place—maybe another user is halfway through an apply—my command waits or fails with a message that the state file is locked. That stops you from applying changes until the ongoing operation completes or is canceled.

Lock Prevention

Now let us consider that there are two teammates, Alice and Bob, who share the code for the publishing application in a Git repository. Here, each checks out the project locally and sets up credentials for AWS. Both have the same remote state configuration. Alice decides to scale up an instance in the production environment, running:

```
opentofu plan
opentofu apply
```

As soon as the apply starts, OpenTofu writes a lock entry to the **publishing-state-lock** DynamoDB table. Meanwhile, Bob tries to run a plan or apply that adds a new S3 bucket for manuscripts. Here, Bob's terminal sees an error or warning like:

```
Error: Error locking state: Error acquiring the state lock
Lock Info:
  ...
```

This indicates that the state is locked and Bob must wait or break the lock (which is not recommended unless absolutely necessary). Once Alice's operation finishes, the lock is removed automatically, allowing Bob to proceed with no conflict. As a result, the final state captures both changes accurately, and no partial updates occur.

Resolving Locking Conflicts

If someone's apply command gets stuck or fails abruptly, a stale lock record might remain in DynamoDB. In that scenario, the next user might see a message that the state is locked even though no active process is running. The recommended fix is checking whether there truly is an ongoing operation. If not, a user might run:

```
opentofu force-unlock <LOCK_ID>
```

The **<LOCK_ID>** appears in the error message or can be found in the DynamoDB table. Force-unlocking is a last resort because forcibly removing the lock while another legitimate operation is in progress can lead to partial updates. Usually, waiting for the original operation to finish or cleaning up a crashed process is the safer path.

Sample Program: Simultaneous Changes

Let's say the application includes two key resources: an EC2 instance that processes manuscript submissions and an S3 bucket for storing the files. Alice updates the instance type from **t2.micro** to **t2.small**:

```
resource "aws_instance" "manuscript_processor" {
  ami           = "ami-12345678"
  instance_type = "t2.small"
  tags = {
    Name = "ManuscriptProcessor"
  }
}
```

Bob, on the other hand, wants to add versioning to the S3 bucket:

```
resource "aws_s3_bucket_versioning" "manuscript_versioning" {
  bucket = aws_s3_bucket.manuscript_store.id
  versioning_configuration {
    status = "Enabled"
  }
}
```

Both changes are legitimate, but if they run apply at the same instant without locking, the state file updates from one might overwrite the other. With remote locking, Alice obtains the lock first. Bob's command sees the locked state, waits or fails. After Alice's process finishes, the lock is released, and Bob's next apply picks up the updated instance size from the state file.

Using a remote backend with locking also centralizes the history of the environment. If versioning is enabled on the S3 bucket, older versions of the state file remain stored for potential rollbacks. That feature means each plan and apply updates a new version of the state, and you can revert if something catastrophic occurs. Meanwhile, the DynamoDB lock ensures that only one operation modifies that version at a time. In a large team, this combination fosters confidence that a developer won't accidentally crush another developer's changes, even if merges in the code happen simultaneously.

Summary

To sum up, you learned how the state file tracked every detail of the infrastructure that you had created, updated, or removed. You realized that this record in OpenTofu was what tied your code to the actual resources living in the cloud environment. You recognized how local state storage was workable for smaller scenarios, but quickly understood that it led to confusion in multi-person teams or pipelines. You also found that remote backends offered a single, authoritative record of the environment, keeping everyone on the same page and preventing overlooked modifications.

In addition, you noted that drift happened whenever manual changes emerged outside the plan-and-apply cycle, so you saw how the plan command flagged those differences. If you wished to keep such edits, you updated the code; otherwise, you allowed OpenTofu to revert them on apply. You learned that the ability to lock the state remained the key to consistent collaboration, since it stopped two users from overwriting each other's updates. Whenever your environment needed improvements or scaling, you confirmed that only one operation ran at a time, reducing unpredictable merges. Through this chapter, you solidified your understanding that the state mechanism was a foundational part of controlling and refining IaC projects in OpenTofu.

Chapter 7: Building and Deploying Apps

Introduction

In this chapter, you will explore techniques to provision the necessary compute resources for the publishing application, which may include spinning up virtual machines or container-based services that accommodate future growth. You will see how each step shapes the underlying environment and lays a strong foundation for additional enhancements. The process will address resource sizing and possible scaling pathways so that the system remains flexible while handling expanding usage requirements over time. You will connect these practical instructions to a broader vision of how every aspect of the application fits together in an orchestrated manner.

Next, you will then turn attention to configuring storage, covering the creation of an environment that stores manuscripts, user content, or metadata files in a consistent, high-availability setting. You will integrate networking elements, such as subnets, routing, and security rules, so that resources exchange data without exposing vulnerable entry points. Here, you will explore working with database services, allowing robust data handling for anything from user profiles to usage statistics.

Provisioning Compute Resources

When you're working on any project that needs to process data in a scalable way, especially when data is constantly being uploaded or changed, it's important to set up the right computing resources. A lot of teams prefer virtual machines since they give you full control over the operating system, the software you install, and runtime configurations. These virtual machines have become super popular over time, not just for standard server tasks, but also for container hosts, development sandboxes, and other specialized workloads. They're affordable, and you can get them in different sizes and in different regions, so they're a flexible choice for all sorts of applications. In publishing, they might be used for stuff like converting manuscripts, interacting with databases, or integrating with outside services—all of which need to run smoothly and securely.

Now here, a practical way to spin up virtual machines in the publishing application is by defining them in OpenTofu code, typically specifying an image, instance type, and any relevant networking details. One might rely on AWS for these compute resources, using a snippet such as:

```
provider "aws" {
  region = "us-east-1"
}
resource "aws_instance" "publishing_backend" {
  ami           = "ami-12345678"
  instance_type = "t2.micro"
```

```
  tags = {
    Name = "PublishingBackend"
  }
}
```

When we run **opentofu plan,** it processes that file, highlighting what changes will occur. After confirming, **opentofu apply** actually provisions the instance in the designated account. This means each backend server becomes traceable via code, and it simplifies expansions or modifications later on. If the instance requires adjusting for heavier load—by switching from **t2.micro** to **t3.medium**, for instance—a single code edit and a new apply step can handle it consistently.

In addition, certain publishing workflows demand script-driven actions when the instance first boots. That is typically handled by adding a user data property, passing a shell script that retrieves dependencies or configures environment variables.

Consider the following example:

```
resource "aws_instance" "publishing_backend" {
  ami           = "ami-12345678"
  instance_type = "t2.micro"

  user_data = file("scripts/publishing_init.sh")
  tags = {
    Name = "PublishingBackend"
  }
}
```

In the above script file, which might install additional libraries or set environment credentials, one can define tasks such as pulling a repository, launching a service process, or configuring file directories relevant to manuscripts. OpenTofu merges that user data into the instance configuration at creation time, giving predictable results every time a new server is provisioned. If a change is introduced in the script, a subsequent plan typically shows whether an in-place update is possible or if a complete re-creation is needed.

There's also the option of launching multiple instances for load balancing or parallel processing. If you add count or for_each constructs in the resource block, the code can define multiple servers under a single block. It might look something like this:

```
resource "aws_instance" "publishing_backend" {
  count = 2
  ami           = "ami-12345678"
  instance_type = "t2.micro"
  user_data = file("scripts/publishing_init.sh")
  tags = {
    Name = "PublishingBackend-${count.index}"
  }
}
```

When **count = 2**, two identical EC2 instances are created, each identified by an index in the final name. If more capacity is needed, simply raise the count and run an apply. The environment seamlessly adjusts by provisioning additional servers, all following the same patterns for tags, user data, or networking associations.

The networking part also must be considered when provisioning these compute resources. One might attach them to subnets, specify security groups, or enable a public IP if external access is necessary. For instance, associating a subnet might look like:

```
resource "aws_instance" "publishing_backend" {
  ami           = "ami-12345678"
  instance_type = "t2.micro"
  subnet_id     = aws_subnet.pub_subnet.id
  tags = {
    Name = "PublishingBackend"
  }
}
```

That line ensures the instance resides in the subnet identified by **aws_subnet.pub_subnet**, which might be declared earlier in the code or within a networking module. If that module is updated—for example, to switch subnets in a new region—the plan step displays the required changes to move or recreate the instance. Because each aspect is codified, the environment remains consistent across dev, staging, or production, making it simpler to replicate or adapt.

On the operations side, once the instance is active, checking logs or monitoring usage can confirm that the correct processes are running. If a developer or admin needs direct access, the SSH key or login details can be stored in a secure location outside the code. Some teams integrate environment variables or external credential managers to avoid exposing sensitive data in **.tf** files. As soon as the instance stands up, the developer verifies that the publishing app's backend tasks—such as file ingestion, data transformations, or route handling—respond as intended. If adjustments are required, a single update to the resource block can reduce or increase capacity, or reassign the system to a new region that might be closer to the user base.

Configuring Storage

Now here, one might begin by declaring an S3 bucket resource for manuscript files in a **.tf** file. After writing the minimal block, running a plan and then applying deploys a private bucket in the specified region. The name needs to be unique across S3, so it can't duplicate an existing bucket name. If that name is already taken, the plan step indicates an error. One can rename and reapply. Versioning also can be added by defining an extra resource that references the same bucket. It appears as below:

```
resource "aws_s3_bucket_versioning" "versioning_settings" {
  bucket = aws_s3_bucket.manuscript_store.id

  versioning_configuration {
    status = "Enabled"
  }
}
```

When this versioning resource is introduced, it adjusts the bucket to keep multiple iterations of the same object rather than overwriting them. Next time a user uploads a file with the same name, a new version is stored. If one wishes to suspend versioning, changing **status = "Suspended"** in that block and reapplying switches it off. The plan output clarifies whether the adjustment requires a fresh creation or if it can update in place. Typically, it modifies the existing bucket configuration.

If the system needs a policy for restricting read or write access to specific roles, an S3 bucket policy might be introduced as shown below:

```
resource "aws_s3_bucket_policy" "manuscript_policy" {
  bucket = aws_s3_bucket.manuscript_store.id
  policy = data.aws_iam_policy_document.manuscript_iam.json
}
```

```
data "aws_iam_policy_document" "manuscript_iam" {
  statement {
    effect = "Allow"
    actions = [
      "s3:GetObject",
      "s3:PutObject"
    ]
    resources = [
      "${aws_s3_bucket.manuscript_store.arn}/*"
    ]
    principals {
      type        = "AWS"
      identifiers =
["arn:aws:iam::123456789012:role/PublishingRole"]
    }
  }
}
```

Once these blocks are saved in the same folder (or a higher-level structure that OpenTofu reads), a plan identifies what changes are pending: creating the versioning configuration if not already present, attaching a policy, and so forth. An apply step implements them. If the environment already had the bucket, the plan typically updates it to enable versioning. If the policy is new, it's attached in place with no disruption to existing files. Now by capturing those declarations in code, each environment can share the same logic for storing manuscripts. Development might have a smaller test bucket name, while production references the main "my-publishing-manuscripts-123" bucket. This arrangement keeps the workflow consistent whenever new members join or a new environment is spun up. If a requirement arises to rename the bucket or shift it to a different region, editing the resource blocks and applying them ensures everything remains in sync—unless a force replacement is triggered, which the plan output notes beforehand.

Establishing Networking

In any cloud-based application, networking forms the backbone that connects all resources securely and efficiently. And, for our publishing application, establishing a robust network infrastructure ensures that our compute resources can communicate with storage and databases while remaining protected from unauthorized access.

Configuring Virtual Private Cloud

A Virtual Private Cloud (VPC) allows you to provision a logically isolated section of the cloud where you can launch AWS resources in a virtual network that you define. This setup provides complete control over the network configuration, including IP address ranges, subnets, route tables, and network gateways.

Define the VPC

Begin by declaring a VPC resource in your OpenTofu configuration. Specify the CIDR block to define the IP address range for your VPC.

```
resource "aws_vpc" "publishing_vpc" {
  cidr_block           = "10.0.0.0/16"
  enable_dns_support   = true
  enable_dns_hostnames = true
  tags = {
    Name = "PublishingVPC"
  }
}
```

In the above script:

- **cidr_block** sets the IP address range for the VPC.
- **enable_dns_support** and **enable_dns_hostnames** are enabled to allow DNS resolution and hostnames within the VPC.
- Tags help in identifying the VPC within the AWS console.

Create Subnets

Subnets divide the VPC's IP address range into smaller segments. Typically, you create both public and private subnets to separate resources that need internet access from those that don't.

```
resource "aws_subnet" "publishing_public_subnet" {
  vpc_id            = aws_vpc.publishing_vpc.id
  cidr_block        = "10.0.1.0/24"
```

```
  availability_zone = "us-east-1a"
  tags = {
    Name = "PublishingPublicSubnet"
    Tier = "Public"
  }
}
resource "aws_subnet" "publishing_private_subnet" {
  vpc_id            = aws_vpc.publishing_vpc.id
  cidr_block        = "10.0.2.0/24"
  availability_zone = "us-east-1a"
  tags = {
    Name = "PublishingPrivateSubnet"
    Tier = "Private"
  }
}
```

Here:

- **aws_subnet.publishing_public_subnet** is a public subnet with internet access.
- **aws_subnet.publishing_private_subnet** is a private subnet without direct internet access.
- Tags differentiate between public and private subnets.

Internet Gateway and Route Tables

Finally, to enable internet access for public subnets, we need to attach an Internet Gateway to the VPC and then we have to configure a route table.

```
resource "aws_internet_gateway" "publishing_igw" {
  vpc_id = aws_vpc.publishing_vpc.id
  tags = {
    Name = "PublishingIGW"
  }
```

```
}
resource "aws_route_table" "publishing_public_rt" {
  vpc_id = aws_vpc.publishing_vpc.id
  route {
    cidr_block = "0.0.0.0/0"
    gateway_id = aws_internet_gateway.publishing_igw.id
  }
  tags = {
    Name = "PublishingPublicRouteTable"
  }
}
resource "aws_route_table_association"
"publishing_public_rt_assoc" {
  subnet_id      = aws_subnet.publishing_public_subnet.id
  route_table_id = aws_route_table.publishing_public_rt.id
}
```

By doing this, **aws_internet_gateway.publishing_igw** attaches an Internet Gateway to the VPC. The **aws_route_table.publishing_public_rt** defines routes for the public subnet, directing internet-bound traffic through the Internet Gateway, and the **aws_route_table_association.publishing_public_rt_assoc** associates the public route table with the public subnet.

Setting up Security Groups

Think of security groups like your building's virtual doormen — they keep an eye on who's coming in and going out of your resources. If you set them up right, they make sure that only approved traffic can reach your EC2 instances and other resources.

Define Security Groups

Create security groups for different tiers of your application, such as backend servers and databases.

```
resource "aws_security_group" "publishing_backend_sg" {
  name        = "PublishingBackendSG"
```

```
  description = "Allow HTTP and SSH inbound traffic"
  vpc_id      = aws_vpc.publishing_vpc.id
  ingress {
    from_port   = 22
    to_port     = 22
    protocol    = "tcp"
    cidr_blocks = ["0.0.0.0/0"]
  }
  ingress {
    from_port   = 80
    to_port     = 80
    protocol    = "tcp"
    cidr_blocks = ["0.0.0.0/0"]
  }
  egress {
    from_port   = 0
    to_port     = 0
    protocol    = "-1"
    cidr_blocks = ["0.0.0.0/0"]
  }
  tags = {
    Name = "PublishingBackendSG"
  }
}
resource "aws_security_group" "publishing_database_sg" {
  name        = "PublishingDatabaseSG"
  description = "Allow MySQL inbound traffic from backend"
  vpc_id      = aws_vpc.publishing_vpc.id
  ingress {
```

```
    from_port       = 3306
    to_port         = 3306
    protocol        = "tcp"
    security_groups =
[aws_security_group.publishing_backend_sg.id]
  }
  egress {
    from_port   = 0
    to_port     = 0
    protocol    = "-1"
    cidr_blocks = ["0.0.0.0/0"]
  }
  tags = {
    Name = "PublishingDatabaseSG"
  }
}
```

Here, **aws_security_group.publishing_backend_sg** allows inbound SSH (port 22) and HTTP (port 80) traffic from anywhere. The **aws_security_group.publishing_database_sg** permits inbound MySQL (port 3306) traffic only from instances associated with the **publishing_backend_sg**. And, both security groups allow all outbound traffic (**egress**) to ensure that resources can communicate as needed.

Attach Security Groups to EC2

When provisioning EC2 instances, attach the appropriate security group to control access.

```
resource "aws_instance" "publishing_backend" {
  ami           = "ami-12345678"
  instance_type = "t2.micro"
  subnet_id     = aws_subnet.publishing_public_subnet.id
  security_groups =
[aws_security_group.publishing_backend_sg.name]
```

```
  tags = {
    Name = "PublishingBackend"
  }
}
```

In this, the **publishing_backend** instance is placed in the public subnet. It is associated with the **publishing_backend_sg**, allowing SSH and HTTP access.

If you have a database instance, attach the **publishing_database_sg**:

```
resource "aws_instance" "publishing_database" {
  ami           = "ami-87654321"
  instance_type = "t2.micro"
  subnet_id     = aws_subnet.publishing_private_subnet.id
  security_groups =
[aws_security_group.publishing_database_sg.name]
  tags = {
    Name = "PublishingDatabase"
  }
}
```

Here, The **publishing_database** instance is placed in the private subnet, enhancing security by restricting direct internet access. It is associated with the **publishing_database_sg**, which only allows MySQL traffic from the backend security group.

Integrating Networking Components

To ensure seamless communication between your compute resources and other services, integrate networking components such as NAT Gateways for outbound internet access from private subnets.

Create a NAT Gateway

A NAT Gateway allows instances in a private subnet to connect to the internet or other AWS services but prevents the internet from initiating connections with those instances.

```
resource "aws_eip" "publishing_nat_eip" {
```

```
  vpc = true
}
resource "aws_nat_gateway" "publishing_nat_gw" {
  allocation_id = aws_eip.publishing_nat_eip.id
  subnet_id     = aws_subnet.publishing_public_subnet.id
  tags = {
    Name = "PublishingNATGateway"
  }
}
```

Here, **aws_eip.publishing_nat_eip** allocates an Elastic IP for the NAT Gateway, and the **aws_nat_gateway.publishing_nat_gw** creates the NAT Gateway in the public subnet.

Update Route Tables for Private Subnets

Then we need to configure the private subnet's route table to direct internet-bound traffic through the NAT Gateway.

```
resource "aws_route_table" "publishing_private_rt" {
  vpc_id = aws_vpc.publishing_vpc.id
  route {
    cidr_block     = "0.0.0.0/0"
    nat_gateway_id = aws_nat_gateway.publishing_nat_gw.id
  }
  tags = {
    Name = "PublishingPrivateRouteTable"
  }
}
resource "aws_route_table_association"
"publishing_private_rt_assoc" {
  subnet_id      = aws_subnet.publishing_private_subnet.id
  route_table_id = aws_route_table.publishing_private_rt.id
```

```
}
```

Here, the **aws_route_table.publishing_private_rt** defines a route for the private subnet to use the NAT Gateway for internet access, and the **aws_route_table_association.publishing_private_rt_assoc** associates the private route table with the private subnet.

With the above configuration in place, by running the following commands, we will be able to set up the entire networking infrastructure as shown below:

```
opentofu init
opentofu plan
opentofu apply
```

Additional Security Group Rules for enhanced Security

Now here, to further secure your application much better, you can add more specific rules to your security groups. For example, restrict SSH access to specific IP addresses or allow HTTPS traffic.

```
resource "aws_security_group" "publishing_backend_sg" {
  name        = "PublishingBackendSG"
  description = "Allow HTTP and SSH inbound traffic"
  vpc_id      = aws_vpc.publishing_vpc.id
  ingress {
    from_port   = 22
    to_port     = 22
    protocol    = "tcp"
    cidr_blocks = ["203.0.113.0/24"]  # Restrict SSH to
specific IP range
  }
  ingress {
    from_port   = 80
    to_port     = 80
    protocol    = "tcp"
    cidr_blocks = ["0.0.0.0/0"]
```

```
  }
  ingress {
    from_port   = 443
    to_port     = 443
    protocol    = "tcp"
    cidr_blocks = ["0.0.0.0/0"]
  }
  egress {
    from_port   = 0
    to_port     = 0
    protocol    = "-1"
    cidr_blocks = ["0.0.0.0/0"]
  }
  tags = {
    Name = "PublishingBackendSG"
  }
}
```

Here, the SSH access is limited to the **203.0.113.0/24** IP range, enhancing security by preventing unauthorized access. And, the HTTPS traffic (port 443) is allowed alongside HTTP (port 80), enabling secure web traffic.

Scaling and Load Balancing

But as our publishing app grows, you might need to scale up your computing resources and distribute traffic more efficiently. You can use load balancers and auto-scaling groups to manage more traffic and keep everything running smoothly.

- Define the Elastic Load Balancer (ELB)

```
resource "aws_elb" "publishing_elb" {
  name                    = "publishing-elb"
  availability_zones =
[aws_subnet.publishing_public_subnet.availability_zone]
```

```
  security_groups    =
[aws_security_group.publishing_backend_sg.id]
  listener {
    instance_port     = 80
    instance_protocol = "HTTP"
    lb_port           = 80
    lb_protocol       = "HTTP"
  }
  listener {
    instance_port     = 443
    instance_protocol = "HTTPS"
    lb_port           = 443
    lb_protocol       = "HTTPS"
    ssl_certificate_id = "arn:aws:iam::123456789012:server-
certificate/your-ssl-cert"
  }
  health_check {
    target              = "HTTP:80/"
    interval            = 30
    timeout             = 5
    healthy_threshold   = 2
    unhealthy_threshold = 2
  }
  tags = {
    Name = "PublishingELB"
  }
}
```

Here, the **aws_elb.publishing_elb** creates an Elastic Load Balancer that listens on ports 80 (HTTP) and 443 (HTTPS). The **ssl_certificate_id** should reference an existing SSL certificate in AWS IAM, while the **health_check** ensures that only healthy instances receive traffic.

- Create the Auto Scaling Group

To handle varying loads, set up an Auto Scaling Group (ASG) that automatically adjusts the number of EC2 instances based on demand.

```
resource "aws_launch_configuration" "publishing_launch_config"
{
  name          = "publishing-launch-config"
  image_id      = "ami-12345678"
  instance_type = "t2.micro"
  security_groups =
[aws_security_group.publishing_backend_sg.id]
  user_data = file("scripts/publishing_init.sh")
  lifecycle {
    create_before_destroy = true
  }
}
resource "aws_autoscaling_group" "publishing_asg" {
  launch_configuration =
aws_launch_configuration.publishing_launch_config.id
  vpc_zone_identifier  = [module.networking.public_subnet_id]
  min_size             = 1
  max_size             = 5
  target_group_arns = [aws_elb.publishing_elb.arn]
  tag {
    key                 = "Name"
    value               = "PublishingASG"
    propagate_at_launch = true
  }
  health_check_type         = "ELB"
  health_check_grace_period = 300
```

```
  tags = {
    Name = "PublishingASG"
  }
}
```

In the above program,

- **aws_launch_configuration.publishing_launch_config** defines the launch configuration for the ASG, specifying the AMI, instance type, security groups, and user data.
- **aws_autoscaling_group.publishing_asg** creates the ASG with a minimum of 1 instance and a maximum of 5, attaching it to the ELB for load balancing.

Integrating Database Services

Integrating a robust database service is pivotal for managing critical aspects of your publishing application, such as authors, metadata, and publishing workflows. A well-configured database ensures data integrity, scalability, and seamless interaction with other components of your infrastructure. We will learn to add a managed database service, specifically leveraging AWS RDS to handle the data needs of your application. You will configure the database instance, secure it within your VPC, and ensure that your compute resources can interact with it efficiently and securely.

Defining the RDS Instance

Begin by declaring an RDS instance in your OpenTofu configuration. This involves specifying the engine type, instance class, storage, and networking details to ensure it operates within your established VPC securely.

```
resource "aws_db_instance" "publishing_db" {
  identifier              = "publishing-db"
  engine                  = "postgres"
  engine_version          = "13.3"
  instance_class          = "db.t3.medium"
  allocated_storage       = 20
  storage_type            = "gp2"
  name                    = "publishingdb"
```

```
  username                    = "adminuser"
  password                    = "SecurePassword123!"
  parameter_group_name        = "default.postgres13"
  skip_final_snapshot         = true
  publicly_accessible         = false
  vpc_security_group_ids      =
[aws_security_group.publishing_database_sg.id]
  db_subnet_group_name        =
aws_db_subnet_group.publishing_db_subnet_group.name
  multi_az                    = false
  auto_minor_version_upgrade = true
  tags = {
    Name = "PublishingDatabase"
  }
}
```

Creating a DB Subnet Group

Here, the RDS instances must be launched within a DB subnet group, which specifies the subnets in your VPC where the database can reside. Typically, these subnets should be private to enhance security.

```
resource "aws_db_subnet_group" "publishing_db_subnet_group" {
  name       = "publishing-db-subnet-group"
  subnet_ids = [
    aws_subnet.publishing_private_subnet.id,
    aws_subnet.publishing_additional_private_subnet.id
  ]
  tags = {
    Name = "PublishingDBSubnetGroup"
  }
}
```

Managing Database Credentials Securely

Hardcoding credentials in your configuration files is a security risk. Instead, use environment variables or secret management services like AWS Secrets Manager to handle sensitive information as shown below.

- Using AWS Secrets Manager

```
resource "aws_secretsmanager_secret" "publishing_db_secret" {
  name = "publishing-db-secret"
  tags = {
    Name = "PublishingDBSecret"
  }
}
resource "aws_secretsmanager_secret_version"
"publishing_db_secret_version" {
  secret_id     =
aws_secretsmanager_secret.publishing_db_secret.id
  secret_string = jsonencode({
    username = "adminuser"
    password = "SecurePassword123!"
  })
}
```

Here, the **aws_secretsmanager_secret** creates a secret to store database credentials, and the **aws_secretsmanager_secret_version** stores the actual credentials securely.

- Referencing the Secret in RDS

First, modify the RDS instance to retrieve credentials from Secrets Manager.

```
resource "aws_db_instance" "publishing_db" {
  identifier                 = "publishing-db"
  engine                     = "postgres"
  engine_version             = "13.3"
  instance_class             = "db.t3.medium"
  allocated_storage          = 20
```

```
  storage_type                = "gp2"
  name                        = "publishingdb"
  username                    = "adminuser"
  password                    =
aws_secretsmanager_secret_version.publishing_db_secret_version
.secret_string["password"]
  parameter_group_name    = "default.postgres13"
  skip_final_snapshot     = true
  publicly_accessible     = false
  vpc_security_group_ids  =
[aws_security_group.publishing_database_sg.id]
  db_subnet_group_name    =
aws_db_subnet_group.publishing_db_subnet_group.name
  multi_az                = false
  auto_minor_version_upgrade = true
  tags = {
    Name = "PublishingDatabase"
  }
}
```

Now here, do ensure that your IAM roles allow OpenTofu to access Secrets Manager.

Enhancing Database Security with IAM Roles

You can use IAM roles with your EC2 instances to give them secure access to AWS services without needing to embed credentials.

```
resource "aws_iam_role" "publishing_backend_role" {
  name = "PublishingBackendRole"
  assume_role_policy = jsonencode({
    Version = "2012-10-17"
    Statement = [{
      Action = "sts:AssumeRole"
      Effect = "Allow"
```

```
      Principal = {
        Service = "ec2.amazonaws.com"
      }
    }]
  })
  tags = {
    Name = "PublishingBackendRole"
  }
}
resource "aws_iam_role_policy" "publishing_backend_policy" {
  name = "PublishingBackendPolicy"
  role = aws_iam_role.publishing_backend_role.id
  policy = jsonencode({
    Version = "2012-10-17"
    Statement = [
      {
        Action = [
          "secretsmanager:GetSecretValue"
        ]
        Effect   = "Allow"
        Resource =
aws_secretsmanager_secret.publishing_db_secret.arn
      }
    ]
  })
}
resource "aws_iam_instance_profile"
"publishing_backend_profile" {
  name = "PublishingBackendProfile"
  role = aws_iam_role.publishing_backend_role.name
```

```
}
```

Next, we modify the backend EC2 instances to utilize the IAM instance profile for secure access to the database credentials.

```
resource "aws_instance" "publishing_backend" {
  ami                          = "ami-12345678"
  instance_type                = "t2.micro"
  subnet_id                    =
aws_subnet.publishing_public_subnet.id
  iam_instance_profile   =
aws_iam_instance_profile.publishing_backend_profile.name
  security_groups            =
[aws_security_group.publishing_backend_sg.name]
  user_data                    = file("scripts/publishing_init.sh")
  tags = {
    Name = "PublishingBackend"
  }
}
```

Creating the Database Schema

We then define the necessary tables to manage authors, metadata, and publishing workflows.

```
CREATE TABLE authors (
    id SERIAL PRIMARY KEY,
    name VARCHAR(100) NOT NULL,
    email VARCHAR(100) UNIQUE NOT NULL,
    bio TEXT
);
CREATE TABLE manuscripts (
    id SERIAL PRIMARY KEY,
    title VARCHAR(200) NOT NULL,
    author_id INTEGER REFERENCES authors(id),
```

```
    submission_date TIMESTAMP DEFAULT CURRENT_TIMESTAMP,
    status VARCHAR(50) DEFAULT 'submitted',
    content TEXT
);
CREATE TABLE workflows (
    id SERIAL PRIMARY KEY,
    manuscript_id INTEGER REFERENCES manuscripts(id),
    step VARCHAR(100),
    completed BOOLEAN DEFAULT FALSE,
    updated_at TIMESTAMP DEFAULT CURRENT_TIMESTAMP
);
```

Connecting Application to Database

Ensure your application can connect to the PostgreSQL database using the credentials fetched from Secrets Manager.

```
database:
  host: "publishing-db.c9akciq32.rds.amazonaws.com"
  port: 5432
  name: "publishingdb"
  user: "${DB_USERNAME}"
  password: "${DB_PASSWORD}"
```

After this, once the above resources are defined, we can now proceed to provision the database services. By defining the RDS instance, configuring subnet groups, securing access through security groups and IAM roles, you establish a robust foundation for handling authors, metadata, and publishing workflows.

Summary

With this, you learned to build and deploy the publishing application by methodically provisioning compute resources, configuring storage, establishing secure networking, and integrating robust database services. In provisioning compute resources, you utilized EC2 instances defined through OpenTofu code, enabling scalable and maintainable backend processing for tasks such as manuscript processing and data integration.

Additionally, you configured storage using S3 buckets with versioning to effectively manage manuscript files, ensuring data integrity and easy rollback capabilities. You defined VPCs, subnets, route tables, and load balancers to create an isolated and secure environment for your application components. Next, with the integration of AWS RDS for database services, you set up a PostgreSQL instance, secured it with appropriate security groups and IAM roles, and implemented automated schema migrations to manage authors, metadata, and publishing workflows efficiently. Through these steps, you achieved a fully operational, secure, and scalable publishing platform, adhering to Infrastructure as Code best practices and ensuring seamless collaboration and maintenance across your development and production environments.

Chapter 8: Organizing and Managing Workspaces

Introduction

In this chapter, you will delve into the essential concept of workspaces within OpenTofu, understanding how they can streamline the management of different environments for your infrastructure projects. You will begin by exploring what workspaces are, gaining a clear understanding of how they allow you to maintain separate state files for various environments such as development, staging, and production. This foundational knowledge will set the stage for effectively managing multiple environments without conflicts or overlaps.

Next, you will learn how to switch between workspaces seamlessly, enabling you to toggle between different configurations and states with ease. This section will provide practical guidance on using OpenTofu commands to create, select, and manage workspaces, ensuring that your workflow remains efficient and organized. You will also explore environment-specific variables, discovering how to tailor configurations for each workspace to meet the unique requirements of different deployment stages. This customization ensures that each environment operates with the appropriate settings and resources, enhancing both flexibility and control.

Finally, the chapter will present workspace best practices, offering strategies to optimize your workspace management for scalability and maintainability. You will learn how to structure your projects, naming conventions, and version control practices to support robust and error-free deployments. By the end of this chapter, you will be equipped with the knowledge and skills to effectively organize and manage workspaces, ensuring that your infrastructure remains consistent, secure, and adaptable across all environments.

Through these topics, you will master the art of workspace management in OpenTofu, enabling you to handle complex infrastructure deployments with confidence and precision.

What Are Workspaces?

Understanding Workspaces

In OpenTofu, the workspaces serve as isolated environments within a single configuration, allowing you to manage multiple deployments of your infrastructure without interference. Each workspace maintains its own state file, which tracks the resources associated with that particular environment. Imagine you are developing a publishing application that handles manuscript submissions, author management, and publishing workflows. During the development lifecycle, you typically work across different environments:

1. **Development (dev):** Where new features are built and tested.
2. **Staging:** A replica of the production environment for final testing before release.
3. **Production (prod):** The live environment serving end-users.

With Workspaces, managing these environments within a single OpenTofu configuration becomes seamless. Each workspace—**dev**, **staging**, and **prod**—can have its own set of resources, variables, and configurations tailored to its specific needs.

Sample Program: Separating Environments with Workspaces

To understand better, let us consider a practical scenario where you need to deploy the application in three environments: development, staging, and production. Each of these environment requires different configurations, such as varying instance sizes, database credentials, and resource limits.

Initialize Default Workspace

When you first initialize OpenTofu in your project directory, it creates a default workspace. This workspace can be used for one of your environments, such as development.

```
opentofu init
```

This command sets up the initial state file (**terraform.tfstate**) within the default workspace, typically named **default**. However, to maintain clarity and organization, it's better to create distinct workspaces for each environment.

Creating Separate Workspaces

Create separate workspaces for **dev**, **staging**, and **prod** using the **opentofu workspace new** command.

```
opentofu workspace new dev
opentofu workspace new staging
opentofu workspace new prod
```

Each command creates a new workspace with its own state file, such as **dev.tfstate**, **staging.tfstate**, and **prod.tfstate**. These state files are stored separately, ensuring that changes in one workspace do not affect the others.

Switching between Workspaces

To work within a specific environment, switch to the corresponding workspace using the **opentofu workspace select** command.

```
opentofu workspace select dev
```

Now, any OpenTofu commands you run—like **plan** or **apply**—will affect only the resources within the **dev** workspace. Similarly, you can switch to **staging** or **prod** as needed.

```
opentofu workspace select staging
```

This kind of flexibility lets you move between environments easily, testing changes in development before moving them to staging and finally to production.

Environment-specific Configurations

Each of these workspaces can have environment-specific variables and configurations. For example, you might use different instance types or database sizes across environments as shown below:

For example, below is the sample Variables File (variables.tf):

```
variable "instance_type" {
  description = "Type of EC2 instance"
  type        = string
}
variable "db_username" {
  description = "Database admin username"
  type        = string
}
variable "db_password" {
  description = "Database admin password"
  type        = string
  sensitive   = true
}
```

You can also create separate variable files for each workspace, such as **`dev.tfvars`**, **`staging.tfvars`**, and **`prod.tfvars`**.

For example, below are the sample separate variable files:

- dev.tfvars

```
instance_type = "t2.micro"
db_username   = "dev_admin"
db_password   = "DevSecurePass123!"
```

- staging.tfvars

```
instance_type = "t2.medium"
db_username   = "staging_admin"
db_password   = "StagingSecurePass123!"
```

- prod.tfvars

```
instance_type = "t3.large"
db_username   = "prod_admin"
db_password   = "ProdSecurePass123!"
```

Now, when applying configurations, we need to specify the appropriate variable file for the current workspace.

```
opentofu apply -var-file=dev.tfvars
```

This ensures that each environment uses its designated settings, maintaining consistency and preventing configuration drift.

Managing Resources across Workspaces

Suppose your publishing application includes EC2 instances, S3 buckets, and RDS databases. You can define these resources in your OpenTofu configuration, and their attributes can vary based on the workspace.

Below is a quick sample of EC2 Instance Configuration (main.tf):

```
provider "aws" {
  region = "us-east-1"
}
resource "aws_instance" "publishing_backend" {
  ami           = "ami-0abcdef1234567890"
  instance_type = var.instance_type
  subnet_id     = module.networking.public_subnet_id
  tags = {
    Name = "PublishingBackend-${opentofu.workspace()}"
  }
```

```
}
```

Here, the **instance_type** is dynamically set based on the workspace-specific variable, and the instance name includes the workspace name for easy identification.

Advanced Workspace Management

As your infrastructure grows, you might encounter more complex scenarios requiring advanced workspace management techniques.

Using Modules with Workspaces

Encapsulate reusable infrastructure components into modules and parameterize them based on the workspace. For instance, you can create a networking module that adjusts subnet sizes or security rules based on the environment.

Below is a Networking Module example (modules/networking/main.tf):

```
variable "environment" {
  description = "The environment for the deployment"
  type        = string
}
variable "vpc_cidr" {
  description = "The CIDR block for the VPC"
  type        = string
}
resource "aws_vpc" "this" {
  cidr_block           = var.vpc_cidr
  enable_dns_support   = true
  enable_dns_hostnames = true
  tags = {
    Name = "PublishingVPC-${var.environment}"
  }
}
# Additional networking resources...
```

Now, next let us use the Module in Root Configuration:

```
module "networking" {
  source      = "./modules/networking"
  environment = opentofu.workspace()
  vpc_cidr    = var.vpc_cidr
}
# Other resources that depend on the networking module...
```

This setup allows each workspace to utilize the networking module with parameters tailored to its specific environment, promoting reuse and reducing duplication in your configuration.

Dynamic Workspace Initialization

Leverage scripts or automation tools to initialize and configure workspaces dynamically based on deployment needs. For example, a script can create new workspaces for feature branches or temporary testing environments, apply configurations, and clean them up after use.

Below is a sample Initialization Script (init_workspace.sh):

```
#!/bin/bash
WORKSPACE=$1
if [ -z "$WORKSPACE" ]; then
  echo "Usage: ./init_workspace.sh <workspace_name>"
  exit 1
fi
# Create and select the workspace
opentofu workspace new $WORKSPACE || opentofu workspace select
$WORKSPACE
# Apply configurations with workspace-specific variables
opentofu apply -var-file="vars/${WORKSPACE}.tfvars"
```

Running this above script with a workspace name automates the creation and configuration process, ensuring consistency and saving time.

Switching between Workspaces

Switching Workspaces Overview

In OpenTofu, switching between workspaces is key to handling different environments like development, staging, and production. If you manage your workspaces right, you can keep each environment separate and prevent any conflicts. That way, the integrity of your infrastructure stays intact. So let's dive in. Here, we will try to seamlessly switch between workspaces using the publishing application example we mentioned earlier. You will also learn how to manage state files and handle resources across different environments.

In the previous section, you set up three distinct workspaces: **dev**, **staging**, and **prod**. Each workspace represents a separate environment with its own configurations and resources. Each workspace has its own state file, such as **dev.tfstate**, **staging.tfstate**, and **prod.tfstate**, ensuring that changes in one workspace do not impact the others.

Switching between Workspaces

To effectively manage resources across multiple workspaces, you must know how to switch between them. OpenTofu provides straightforward commands to create, select, and list workspaces.

Listing Available Workspaces

Before switching, it's useful to see all available workspaces.

```
opentofu workspace list
```

Given below is the sample output:

```
 * default
   dev
   staging
   prod
```

The asterisk (*) indicates the currently active workspace. Initially, when you run **opentofu init**, it creates the **default** workspace.

Creating a New Workspace

If you need additional environments or workspaces, create them using:

```
opentofu workspace new <workspace_name>
```

Following is a quick example:

```
opentofu workspace new testing
```

This command creates a new workspace named **`testing`** with its own state file (**`testing.tfstate`**).

Selecting a Workspace

Now here, to switch to a different workspace, use:

```
opentofu workspace select <workspace_name>
```

For example:

```
opentofu workspace select staging
```

Upon selection, any subsequent OpenTofu commands (**`plan`**, **`apply`**, etc.) will operate within the **`staging`** workspace.

Automating Workspace Selection

For streamlined workflows, especially in team environments or CI/CD pipelines, automate workspace selection within scripts or configuration files. For example, in a deployment script:

```
#!/bin/bash
# Usage: ./deploy.sh <workspace> <var_file>
WORKSPACE=$1
VAR_FILE=$2
# Check if workspace exists, create if not
if ! opentofu workspace list | grep -q "^  $WORKSPACE$"; then
  opentofu workspace new $WORKSPACE
fi
# Select the workspace
opentofu workspace select $WORKSPACE
# Apply the configuration with the specified variable file
opentofu apply -var-file="$VAR_FILE"
```

This script ensures that the specified workspace exists, selects it, and applies the configuration using the appropriate variable file.

Managing State across Workspaces

Each workspace maintains its own state file, isolating the resources managed within that environment. Proper management of these state files is crucial for maintaining consistency and avoiding conflicts.

Understanding State Isolation

When you switch to a different workspace, OpenTofu automatically references the corresponding state file.

For example, switching to **`prod`** will use **`prod.tfstate`**, keeping the production resources separate from development or staging resources.

Viewing Current State

To inspect the current state of a workspace, you can use:

```
opentofu show
```

This command displays the resources tracked by the current workspace's state file, helping you verify that the correct resources are managed within each environment.

Moving Resources between Workspaces

In some cases, you might need to move resources from one workspace to another. OpenTofu does not provide a direct command for this, but you can achieve it through the following steps:

- Export the resource from the source workspace

```
opentofu workspace select dev
opentofu state show aws_instance.publishing_backend >
backend.json
```

- Import the Resource into the Target Workspace

```
opentofu workspace select staging
opentofu import aws_instance.publishing_backend backend.json
```

- Verify the Import

```
opentofu show
```

Just remember that this process requires careful handling to ensure that dependencies and references are maintained correctly.

Environment-specific Variables

Introduction to Environment-specific Variables

Environment-specific variables in OpenTofu enable you to define distinct settings, such as instance sizes, database credentials, and resource limits, ensuring that each environment operates optimally and securely. This section will take you through the practical steps of configuring and managing environment-specific variables, building upon the workspace management techniques learned earlier.

Previously, you learned about workspaces such as **`dev`**, **`staging`**, and **`prod`**—each have their own state files and can be managed independently. This isolation is crucial for deploying infrastructure changes safely and consistently across different stages of your application lifecycle. Here, you will extend this knowledge by configuring environment-specific variables. These variables enable you to adjust resource configurations, credentials, and other settings based on the active workspace.

Creating Workspace-specific Variable files

We begin with creating separate variable files for each workspace. These files will contain the specific values for each environment, allowing you to customize configurations without altering the main configuration files.

Following is the directory structure:

```
publishing-app/
├── main.tf
├── variables.tf
├── backend.tf
├── dev.tfvars
├── staging.tfvars
├── prod.tfvars
├── modules/
│   └── networking/
│       ├── main.tf
│       ├── variables.tf
│       └── outputs.tf
├── scripts/
```

```
│   └── init_workspace.sh
└── README.md
```

Given below is the dev.tfvars:

```
instance_type       = "t2.micro"
db_instance_class   = "db.t3.micro"
db_username         = "dev_admin"
db_password         = "DevSecurePass123!"
allowed_ssh_cidrs   = ["203.0.113.0/24"]  # Replace with your
development IP range
```

Given below is the staging.tfvars:

```
instance_type       = "t2.medium"
db_instance_class   = "db.t3.medium"
db_username         = "staging_admin"
db_password         = "StagingSecurePass123!"
allowed_ssh_cidrs   = ["198.51.100.0/24"]  # Replace with your
staging IP range
```

Given below is the prod.tfvars:

```
instance_type       = "t3.large"
db_instance_class   = "db.t3.large"
db_username         = "prod_admin"
db_password         = "ProdSecurePass123!"
allowed_ssh_cidrs   = ["192.0.2.0/24"]  # Replace with your
production IP range
```

In the above, each **.tfvars** file provides specific values for variables defined in **variables.tf**. The **instance_type** and **db_instance_class** are scaled up from **dev** to **prod** to handle increased load and performance requirements. The **db_username** and **db_password** are unique for each environment to enhance security. And, the **allowed_ssh_cidrs** are tailored to restrict SSH access to IP ranges appropriate for each environment.

Applying Workspace-specific Variables

Now, when you are trying to deploy resources to a specific workspace, try to reference the corresponding variable file in order to ensure that environment-specific configurations are applied.

See the following example:

- Deploying to Development:

```
# Select dev workspace
opentofu workspace select dev
# Apply configurations with dev variables
opentofu apply -var-file=dev.tfvars
```

- Deploying to Staging:

```
# Select staging workspace
opentofu workspace select staging
# Apply configurations with staging variables
opentofu apply -var-file=staging.tfvars
```

- Deploying to Production:

```
# Select prod workspace
opentofu workspace select prod
# Apply configurations with prod variables
opentofu apply -var-file=prod.tfvars
```

In the above program, the **opentofu apply -var-file=<file>** applies the configuration using the specified variable file, ensuring that each environment uses its designated settings.

Integrating Variables into Resource Definitions

In your main configuration files, you need to reference the defined variables to customize resource properties based on the active workspace.

See the following script:

```
provider "aws" {
  region = "us-east-1"
```

```
}
module "networking" {
  source = "./modules/networking"
  # Pass necessary variables
}
resource "aws_instance" "publishing_backend" {
  ami           = "ami-0abcdef1234567890"  # Replace with your
AMI ID
  instance_type = var.instance_type
  subnet_id     = module.networking.public_subnet_id
  tags = {
    Name = "PublishingBackend-${opentofu.workspace()}"
  }
}
resource "aws_db_instance" "publishing_db" {
  identifier              = "publishing-db-
${opentofu.workspace()}"
  engine                  = "postgres"
  engine_version          = "13.3"
  instance_class          = var.db_instance_class
  allocated_storage       = 20
  storage_type            = "gp2"
  name                    = "publishingdb"
  username                = var.db_username
  password                = var.db_password
  parameter_group_name    = "default.postgres13"
  skip_final_snapshot     = true
  publicly_accessible     = false
  vpc_security_group_ids  =
[aws_security_group.publishing_database_sg.id]
```

```
  db_subnet_group_name     =
aws_db_subnet_group.publishing_db_subnet_group.name
  multi_az                 = false
  auto_minor_version_upgrade = true
  tags = {
    Name = "PublishingDatabase-${opentofu.workspace()}"
  }
}
resource "aws_security_group" "publishing_backend_sg" {
  name        = "PublishingBackendSG-${opentofu.workspace()}"
  description = "Allow HTTP, HTTPS, and SSH inbound traffic
for ${opentofu.workspace()}"
  vpc_id      = module.networking.vpc_id
  ingress {
    from_port   = 22
    to_port     = 22
    protocol    = "tcp"
    cidr_blocks = var.allowed_ssh_cidrs
  }
  ingress {
    from_port   = 80
    to_port     = 80
    protocol    = "tcp"
    cidr_blocks = ["0.0.0.0/0"]
  }
  ingress {
    from_port   = 443
    to_port     = 443
    protocol    = "tcp"
    cidr_blocks = ["0.0.0.0/0"]
```

```
  }
  egress {
    from_port   = 0
    to_port     = 0
    protocol    = "-1"
    cidr_blocks = ["0.0.0.0/0"]
  }
  tags = {
    Name = "PublishingBackendSG-${opentofu.workspace()}"
  }
}
```

Here, the **opentofu.workspace()** dynamically inserts the current workspace name into resource identifiers and tags, ensuring uniqueness across environments. The **var.instance_type** and **var.db_instance_class** customizes the instance types based on the active workspace. And, the **var.allowed_ssh_cidrs** restricts the SSH access to specific IP ranges appropriate for each environment.

Managing Variable Files with Modules

When your infrastructure gets bigger, making your configurations modular makes them easier to reuse and maintain. You can create modules that accept variables, allowing different environments to supply their specific configurations as shown below:

```
variable "vpc_cidr" {
  description = "The CIDR block for the VPC"
  type        = string
}
variable "public_subnet_cidr" {
  description = "The CIDR block for the public subnet"
  type        = string
}
variable "private_subnet_cidr" {
  description = "The CIDR block for the private subnet"
```

```
  type        = string
}
variable "availability_zone" {
  description = "The availability zone for the subnets"
  type        = string
}
resource "aws_vpc" "this" {
  cidr_block           = var.vpc_cidr
  enable_dns_support   = true
  enable_dns_hostnames = true
  tags = {
    Name = "PublishingVPC-${opentofu.workspace()}"
  }
}
resource "aws_subnet" "public" {
  vpc_id            = aws_vpc.this.id
  cidr_block        = var.public_subnet_cidr
  availability_zone = var.availability_zone
  tags = {
    Name = "PublishingPublicSubnet-${opentofu.workspace()}"
    Tier = "Public"
  }
}
resource "aws_subnet" "private" {
  vpc_id            = aws_vpc.this.id
  cidr_block        = var.private_subnet_cidr
  availability_zone = var.availability_zone
  tags = {
    Name = "PublishingPrivateSubnet-${opentofu.workspace()}"
```

```
    Tier = "Private"
  }
}
output "vpc_id" {
  description = "The ID of the VPC"
  value       = aws_vpc.this.id
}
output "public_subnet_id" {
  description = "The ID of the public subnet"
  value       = aws_subnet.public.id
}
output "private_subnet_id" {
  description = "The ID of the private subnet"
  value       = aws_subnet.private.id
}
```

In the above example, the **vpc_cidr, public_subnet_cidr, private_subnet_cidr, availability_zone** variables allow each workspace to specify its networking configurations.

Now, we use the Module in Root Configuration (main.tf):

```
module "networking" {
  source              = "./modules/networking"
  vpc_cidr            = var.vpc_cidr
  public_subnet_cidr  = var.public_subnet_cidr
  private_subnet_cidr = var.private_subnet_cidr
  availability_zone   = var.availability_zone
}
```

We then include networking variables in each workspace's .tfvars file. For example:

```
vpc_cidr            = "10.0.0.0/16"
public_subnet_cidr  = "10.0.1.0/24"
```

```
private_subnet_cidr = "10.0.2.0/24"
availability_zone   = "us-east-1a"
instance_type       = "t2.micro"
db_instance_class   = "db.t3.micro"
db_username         = "dev_admin"
db_password         = "DevSecurePass123!"
allowed_ssh_cidrs   = ["203.0.113.0/24"]
```

If you learn to adapt to the specific variables in different environments, your infrastructure deployments will be consistent, secure, and tailored to meet each environment's unique needs.

Summary

In a nutshell, you dug into the basic idea of workspaces and got how they help with keeping different environments, like development, staging, and production, separate and organized. You learned what workspaces are and how they keep state files separate, so changes in one environment don't accidentally mess up the others. You also learned how to create, select, and switch between workspaces using practical examples, like deploying a publishing application across different environments.

Then, it moved on to managing environment-specific variables, showing how to set up different settings for each workspace. You got to try things out for yourself, like defining variables, making workspace-specific variable files, and adding these variables to resource configurations to personalize how things are deployed. It also covered best practices for managing workspaces, like using consistent naming conventions, automating workspace setup, keeping sensitive data secure, and maintaining version control for configurations. By the time you're done with this chapter, you will have all you need to successfully organize and manage workspaces in OpenTofu.

Chapter 9: Importing and Managing Existing Infrastructure

Introduction

In this chapter, you will learn how to smoothly integrate existing resources into your OpenTofu configurations. So, whether you're switching from another infrastructure as code tool or adding resources that you've created manually, importing lets you put all these assets under OpenTofu's management.

First, you will learn how to figure out which resources are good to import, focusing on the prerequisites needed and figuring out how much of the resources you need to manage. Then, the chapter will walk you through using the import command, explaining its syntax, options, and best practices. We will also give you some practical examples to show you how to do the import process successfully so that your resources are accurately captured in OpenTofu's state files.

After importing resources, it's essential to make sure they're in sync with your configuration files. You will learn how to verify that the imported resources match your desired infrastructure state and how to deal with any inconsistencies that might pop up. The chapter will also cover updating the state after imports, making sure your state files stay accurate and show your current infrastructure. By the time you're done, you will have all the know-how to smoothly import and handle existing infrastructure in OpenTofu.

Identifying Resources to Import

As your infrastructure evolves, you might find yourself managing resources that were initially created outside of OpenTofu. Whether these resources were provisioned manually, by another IaC tool, or by legacy scripts, integrating them into your OpenTofu workflow ensures consistency, maintainability, and centralized management. Here, we will identify which existing resources are suitable for import into OpenTofu, specifically referencing our developed publishing application.

Importance of Importing Resources

Before diving into the technical steps, it's essential to understand why importing existing resources into OpenTofu is beneficial:

1. **Centralized Management:** Consolidates all infrastructure resources under a single IaC tool, simplifying management and oversight.
2. **Consistency:** Ensures that all resources adhere to defined configurations and standards, reducing configuration drift.
3. **Version Control:** Allows infrastructure changes to be tracked, reviewed, and rolled back using version control systems.
4. **Automation:** Enables the automation of deployments, updates, and scaling operations, enhancing efficiency and reducing manual errors.

By importing existing resources, you transition from disparate management methods to a unified,

automated, and scalable infrastructure management approach.

Inventory Existing Infrastructure

The first step in identifying resources to import is conducting a comprehensive inventory of your current infrastructure. For our publishing application, this involves listing all AWS resources that have been provisioned manually or through other tools.

Suppose our publishing application currently has the following resources manually created in AWS:

1. **EC2 Instances:**
   - **`publishing-backend-dev`**
   - **`publishing-backend-staging`**
   - **`publishing-backend-prod`**
2. **RDS Instances:**
   - **`publishing-db-dev`**
   - **`publishing-db-staging`**
   - **`publishing-db-prod`**
3. **S3 Buckets:**
   - **`publishing-assets-dev`**
   - **`publishing-assets-staging`**
   - **`publishing-assets-prod`**
4. **VPC Components:**
   - VPC: **`publishing-vpc`**
   - Subnets: **`publishing-public-subnet`**, **`publishing-private-subnet`**
5. **Security Groups:**
   - **`publishing-backend-sg`**
   - **`publishing-db-sg`**
6. **IAM Roles:**
   - **`publishing-backend-role`**
7. **Load Balancers:**
   - **`publishing-lb-prod`**

8. **Elastic IPs:**
    - **`publishing-eip-prod`**
9. **CloudWatch Alarms:**
    - **`publishing-backend-cpu-high-prod`**

Gather Necessary Information for Each Resource

To successfully import resources, you need to gather specific details about each resource. This information typically includes:

1. **Resource Identifiers:**
    - **EC2:** Instance ID (e.g., **`i-0abcd1234efgh5678`**)
    - **RDS:** DB Instance Identifier (e.g., **`publishing-db-prod`**)
    - **S3:** Bucket Name (e.g., **`publishing-assets-prod`**)
    - **VPC:** VPC ID (e.g., **`vpc-0abc1234def567890`**)
    - **Security Groups:** Security Group ID (e.g., **`sg-0123abcd4567efgh8`**)
    - **IAM Roles:** Role Name or ARN (e.g., **`arn:aws:iam::123456789012:role/publishing-backend-role`**)
    - **Load Balancers:** Load Balancer ARN or Name (e.g., **`publishing-lb-prod`**)
    - **Elastic IPs:** Allocation ID (e.g., **`eipalloc-12345678`**)
    - **CloudWatch Alarms:** Alarm Name (e.g., **`publishing-backend-cpu-high-prod`**)
2. **Resource Configuration Details:**
    - **EC2:** AMI ID, instance type, key pair, security groups, IAM roles, network interfaces.
    - **RDS:** Engine type, version, instance class, storage settings, security groups, subnet group.
    - **S3:** Bucket policies, versioning, access control settings.
    - **VPC:** CIDR blocks, subnet configurations, route tables, internet gateways.
    - **Security Groups:** Inbound and outbound rules.
    - **IAM Roles:** Attached policies, trust relationships.
    - **Load Balancers:** Listener configurations, target groups, security groups.

    - **Elastic IPs:** Association with instances.
    - **CloudWatch Alarms:** Metric details, threshold settings, notification actions.

For the **publishing-db-prod** RDS instance:

- **Resource Identifier: publishing-db-prod**
- **Configuration Details:**
    - **Engine:** PostgreSQL 13.3
    - **Instance Class: db.t3.large**
    - **Storage:** 100 GB, **gp2**
    - **VPC Security Groups: sg-0123abcd4567efgh8**
    - **Subnet Group: publishing-db-subnet-group**
    - **Backup Retention:** 7 days
    - **Multi-AZ:** Enabled

You can gather this info through the AWS Management Console, AWS CLI, or OpenTofu's own data sources.

Prepare OpenTofu Configuration for Imported Resources

Before importing, ensure that your OpenTofu configuration files (**.tf** files) include resource definitions that match the existing resources. This alignment is crucial to prevent discrepancies between OpenTofu's state and the actual resource configurations.

For the **publishing-backend-prod** EC2 instance, your **main.tf** should have a corresponding resource block:

```
resource "aws_instance" "publishing_backend_prod" {
  # Placeholder values; actual values will be imported
  ami             = "ami-placeholder"
  instance_type = "t2.micro"
  subnet_id       = "subnet-placeholder"
  security_groups =
[aws_security_group.publishing_backend_sg.id]
  iam_instance_profile =
aws_iam_instance_profile.publishing_backend_profile.name
  tags = {
```

```
    Name = "publishing-backend-prod"
  }
}
```

In the above, use placeholders for attributes like **ami**, **instance_type**, and **subnet_id** which will be aligned during the import.

Document Dependencies and Order of Imports

Some resources depend on others, requiring a specific order of import to maintain integrity. Documenting these dependencies ensures that you import resources in the correct sequence, preventing errors and ensuring successful integration.

For our publishing application:

1. **VPC and Networking Components:**
   - Import **publishing-vpc**
   - Import **publishing-public-subnet**
   - Import **publishing-private-subnet**
   - Import route tables and gateways
2. **Security Groups:**
   - Import **publishing-backend-sg**
   - Import **publishing-db-sg**
3. **IAM Roles and Profiles:**
   - Import **publishing-backend-role**
   - Import **publishing-backend-profile**
4. **RDS Instances:**
   - Import **publishing-db-prod**
5. **EC2 Instances:**
   - Import **publishing-backend-prod**
6. **Load Balancers:**
   - Import **publishing-lb-prod**
7. **Elastic IPs:**
   - Import **publishing-eip-prod**

8. **CloudWatch Alarms:**
    - Import **`publishing-backend-cpu-high-prod`**

If you document the above order in a checklist or script, you make sure that each resource is imported only after its dependencies are in place.

Backup Current State and Configuration

Before performing any import operations, it is crucial to backup your current OpenTofu state and configuration files. This precaution ensures that you can restore your infrastructure to its previous state in case of any issues during the import process.

1. **Backup State files:**
    - If using remote backends (e.g., S3), ensure that versioning is enabled.
    - Download local state files if using local backends.
2. **Backup Configuration Files:**

```
Make copies of all .tf and .tfvars files.
```

- Store backups in a secure location, preferably outside the main repository.

```
# Create a backup directory
mkdir backups
# Backup state files (if local)
cp *.tfstate backups/
# Backup configuration files
cp *.tf backups/
```

For remote backends, ensure that versioning is enabled to retrieve previous versions if necessary.

Plan and Execute the Import

To plan the import process, you need to figure out the order of resource imports based on dependencies and prepare the necessary OpenTofu commands. Having a step-by-step plan makes sure everything goes smoothly. Following the below steps:

- Import VPC

```
opentofu import aws_vpc.publishing_vpc vpc-0abc1234def567890
```

- Import Subnets

```
opentofu import aws_subnet.publishing_public_subnet subnet-0abcd1234efgh5678
opentofu import aws_subnet.publishing_private_subnet subnet-0abcd1234efgh5679
```

- Import Security Groups

```
opentofu import aws_security_group.publishing_backend_sg sg-0123abcd4567efgh8
opentofu import aws_security_group.publishing_db_sg sg-0123abcd4567efgh9
```

- Import IAM Roles and Profiles

```
opentofu import aws_iam_role.publishing_backend_role arn:aws:iam::123456789012:role/publishing-backend-role
opentofu import aws_iam_instance_profile.publishing_backend_profile arn:aws:iam::123456789012:instance-profile/publishing-backend-profile
```

- Import RDS Instances

```
opentofu import aws_db_instance.publishing_db_prod publishing-db-prod
```

- Import EC2 Instances

```
opentofu import aws_instance.publishing_backend_prod i-0abcd1234efgh5678
```

- Import Load Balancers

```
opentofu import aws_lb.publishing_lb_prod arn:aws:elasticloadbalancing:us-east-1:123456789012:loadbalancer/app/publishing-lb-prod/abcd1234efgh5678
```

- Import Elastic IPs

```
opentofu import aws_eip.publishing_eip_prod eipalloc-12345678
```

- Import CloudWatch Alarms

```
opentofu import
aws_cloudwatch_metric_alarm.publishing_backend_cpu_high_prod
publishing-backend-cpu-high-prod
```

With the above import plans in place, you can then simply execute each import command sequentially. Now here, ensure that you are in the correct workspace (e.g., **prod**) before executing import commands to align the imported resources with the appropriate environment. The resource names in the import commands (**aws_vpc.publishing_vpc**, **aws_instance.publishing_backend_prod**, etc.) must match the resource blocks defined in your OpenTofu configuration files. And make sure to use the exact resource identifiers (e.g., VPC ID, Subnet ID, Security Group ID) as they exist in AWS.

Reconcile and Validate the Import

After importing all desired resources and updating your configuration files, perform a final reconciliation and validation to ensure everything is correctly integrated. To do this,

- Execute opentofu plan to preview any changes that OpenTofu intends to make.
- If the plan shows no unintended changes, proceed to apply the configurations. This step finalizes the import process and integrates the resources into OpenTofu's management.

Following is a quick sample program:

```
# Select the prod workspace
opentofu workspace select prod
# Validate the configuration
opentofu validate
# Generate a plan to verify no unintended changes
opentofu plan -var-file=prod.tfvars
# If the plan looks correct, apply the configuration
opentofu apply -var-file=prod.tfvars
```

In the above script,

- **opentofu validate:** Checks for syntax errors and validates the configuration files.
- **opentofu plan:** Shows the changes that OpenTofu will make. After a successful import and reconciliation, the plan should show no changes unless there are discrepancies.
- **opentofu apply:** Applies the configurations, finalizing the import process.

This whole process not only enhances operational efficiency but also aligns your infrastructure with best practices in IaC.

Reconciliation Post-Import

After successfully importing existing infrastructure resources into OpenTofu, the next critical step is **reconciliation**. Reconciliation ensures that your OpenTofu configuration files accurately reflect the current state of your imported resources. This alignment prevents OpenTofu from making unintended changes during future deployments and maintains consistency between your codebase and the actual infrastructure. Here, we will explore how to identify and resolve configuration mismatches, update your OpenTofu code to align with the imported resources, and implement best practices to maintain this alignment over time.

Understanding Reconciliation

Reconciliation in the context of OpenTofu involves ensuring that the configurations defined in your .tf files match the actual state of the resources in your cloud provider. Post-import, discrepancies can arise due to:

1. The imported resource may have attributes not defined in your OpenTofu files.

```
Placeholder values or incorrect configurations in the .tf
files can lead to conflicts.
```

2. Certain attributes might be managed outside of OpenTofu, causing unexpected differences.

Reconciliation addresses these issues by aligning your OpenTofu configurations with the real-world state of your infrastructure, ensuring seamless management and avoiding unintended modifications.

Identify Configuration Mismatches

The first step in reconciliation is to identify any mismatches between your OpenTofu configuration files and the actual state of the imported resources. This identification can be achieved using the **`opentofu plan`** command, which compares the desired state (as defined in your **`.tf`** files) with the current state (as recorded in the state file).

```
opentofu plan -var-file=prod.tfvars
```

The plan may output actions indicating that certain attributes need to be updated. For example:

```
# aws_instance.publishing_backend_prod will be updated in-
place
```

```
~ resource "aws_instance" "publishing_backend_prod" {
      ami           = "ami-placeholder" => "ami-
0abcdef1234567890"
      instance_type = "t2.micro"        => "t3.large"
      subnet_id     = "subnet-placeholder" => "subnet-
0abcd1234efgh5678"
  }
# aws_db_instance.publishing_db_prod will be updated in-place
~ resource "aws_db_instance" "publishing_db_prod" {
      instance_class = "db.t3.micro" => "db.t3.large"
  }
```

This above script will also show which attributes are mismatched and what changes OpenTofu intends to make.

Update OpenTofu Configuration files

Now to resolve these mismatches, update your OpenTofu configuration files (**`.tf`** files) to reflect the actual attributes of the imported resources. This alignment ensures that OpenTofu recognizes the current state and does not attempt unnecessary modifications.

First, update the EC2 Instance Configuration:

```
resource "aws_instance" "publishing_backend_prod" {
  ami           = "ami-0abcdef1234567890"      # Updated to
actual AMI
  instance_type = "t3.large"                    # Updated to
actual instance type
  subnet_id     = "subnet-0abcd1234efgh5678"   # Updated to
actual subnet ID
  security_groups =
[aws_security_group.publishing_backend_sg.id]
  iam_instance_profile =
aws_iam_instance_profile.publishing_backend_profile.name
  tags = {
    Name = "publishing-backend-prod"
```

```
  }
}
```

Then, update the RDS Database Configuration:

```
resource "aws_db_instance" "publishing_db_prod" {
  identifier                = "publishing-db-prod"
  engine                    = "postgres"
  engine_version            = "13.3"
  instance_class            = "db.t3.large"          # Updated
to actual instance class
  allocated_storage         = 100
  storage_type              = "gp2"
  name                      = "publishingdb-prod"
  username                  = "prod_admin"
  password                  = "ProdSecurePass123!"   # Consider
using variables or secrets
  parameter_group_name      = "default.postgres13"
  skip_final_snapshot       = true
  publicly_accessible       = false
  vpc_security_group_ids    =
[aws_security_group.publishing_db_sg.id]
  db_subnet_group_name      =
aws_db_subnet_group.publishing_db_subnet_group.name
  multi_az                  = false
  auto_minor_version_upgrade = true
  tags = {
    Name = "publishing-db-prod"
  }
}
```

Now here, while you do all these changes, I advise you to manage sensitive attributes like password using variables or integrating with secret management services to enhance security.

Utilizing 'opentofu fmt' and 'opentofu validate'

After you update your configuration files, it's a good idea to format and validate them. This helps make sure there are no syntax errors and that they follow best practices.

```
# Format the configuration files
opentofu fmt
# Validate the configuration
opentofu validate
```

Given below is the expected output:

```
Success! The configuration is valid.
```

A successful validation indicates that your configurations are syntactically correct and logically consistent.

Next, after updating and validating your configuration files, run a **plan** to verify that OpenTofu no longer detects discrepancies between your configurations and the actual resource states.

```
opentofu plan -var-file=prod.tfvars
```

Given below is the expected output:

```
No changes. Infrastructure is up-to-date.
```

Here, **No Changes** indicates that OpenTofu recognizes the current state as fully aligned with your configuration files, signifying successful reconciliation. And if there are changes, it will show the output as **If Changes Are Detected.** If you get this as the output, then you need to review the plan output to identify any remaining discrepancies and address them accordingly.

Automating Reconciliation Processes

Here, in order to streamline reconciliation and maintain consistency across your infrastructure, you may consider automating the reconciliation checks and updates using the CI/CD pipelines and automated scripts as below:

Following is the GitHub Actions Workflow program:

```
jobs:
  reconcile:
    runs-on: ubuntu-latest
```

```
    steps:
      - name: Checkout Code
        uses: actions/checkout@v2
      - name: Set up OpenTofu
        uses: hashicorp/setup-opentofu@v1
        with:
          opentofu_version: "latest"
      - name: Configure AWS Credentials
        uses: aws-actions/configure-aws-credentials@v1
        with:
          aws-access-key-id: ${{ secrets.AWS_ACCESS_KEY_ID }}
          aws-secret-access-key: ${{
secrets.AWS_SECRET_ACCESS_KEY }}
          aws-region: us-east-1
      - name: Initialize OpenTofu
        run: opentofu init
      - name: Select Workspace
        run: opentofu workspace select prod
      - name: Validate Configuration
        run: opentofu validate
      - name: Plan Infrastructure
        run: opentofu plan -var-file=vars/prod.tfvars -
out=plan.out
      - name: Apply if No Changes Detected
        run: |
          if opentofu show -no-color plan.out | grep -q "No
changes."; then
            echo "No drift detected."
          else
            echo "Drift detected. Applying changes."
```

```
            opentofu apply plan.out
          fi
```

And the following is the Cron Job script:

```
#!/bin/bash
# Navigate to OpenTofu project directory
cd /path/to/publishing-app
# Initialize OpenTofu
opentofu init
# Select the prod workspace
opentofu workspace select prod
# Run a plan and capture output
opentofu plan -var-file=prod.tfvars -out=plan.out
# Check if the plan indicates changes
if opentofu show -no-color plan.out | grep -q "No changes.";
then
  echo "$(date): No drift detected."
else
  echo "$(date): Drift detected. Applying changes."
  opentofu apply -auto-approve plan.out
fi
```

Troubleshooting Reconciliation Issues

Despite careful planning, reconciliation may encounter issues. For example, after importing the **publishing-db-prod** RDS instance, OpenTofu plans to change the **allocated_storage** from **100** to **200**.

Given below is the plan output:

```
# aws_db_instance.publishing_db_prod will be updated in-place
~ resource "aws_db_instance" "publishing_db_prod" {
      allocated_storage = 100 => 200
```

```
  }
```

To resolve, we can verify if the RDS instance currently has 100 GB or 200 GB allocated. If the actual storage is 200 GB, then try to update main.tf:

```
resource "aws_db_instance" "publishing_db_prod" {
  identifier                 = "publishing-db-prod"
  engine                     = "postgres"
  engine_version             = "13.3"
  instance_class             = "db.t3.large"
  allocated_storage          = 200                    # Updated to
actual storage
  storage_type               = "gp2"
  name                       = "publishingdb-prod"
  username                   = "prod_admin"
  password                   = "ProdSecurePass123!"
  parameter_group_name       = "default.postgres13"
  skip_final_snapshot        = true
  publicly_accessible        = false
  vpc_security_group_ids     =
[aws_security_group.publishing_db_sg.id]
  db_subnet_group_name       =
aws_db_subnet_group.publishing_db_subnet_group.name
  multi_az                   = false
  auto_minor_version_upgrade = true
  tags = {
    Name = "publishing-db-prod"
  }
}
```

Then run the plan again.

```
opentofu plan -var-file=prod.tfvars
```

Reconciliation post-import is vital. It ensures that your OpenTofu configurations accurately represent your existing infrastructure. To maintain consistency and leverage OpenTofu's full capabilities for infrastructure management, you must meticulously identify mismatches, update configuration files, address dependencies, and adhere to best practices. Our publishing application is a practical example of how to navigate the complexities of reconciliation. It ensures that your imported resources are seamlessly integrated into your OpenTofu workflows.

Updating State after Imports

After successfully importing existing infrastructure resources and reconciling your OpenTofu configuration files, the next critical step is **updating and finalizing the state file**. This process ensures that OpenTofu's state accurately reflects your current infrastructure, allowing for seamless future management and deployments. The state file in OpenTofu serves as a single source of truth for your infrastructure. It maps your configuration files to the actual resources in your cloud provider, tracking their current state.

After importing resources, updating the state file is essential to:

- Align the state file with the actual infrastructure, preventing OpenTofu from making unnecessary or unintended changes.
- Allow OpenTofu to accurately manage, update, or destroy resources based on the state file.
- Maintain synchronization between your IaC configurations and the real-world state of your infrastructure.

Review Imported Resources in the State File

Before making any changes, it's crucial to review the current state of your imported resources to ensure they have been correctly added to OpenTofu's state.

```
opentofu state list
```

Given below is the expected output:

```
aws_instance.publishing_backend_prod
aws_db_instance.publishing_db_prod
aws_security_group.publishing_backend_sg
aws_security_group.publishing_db_sg
aws_vpc.publishing_vpc
aws_subnet.publishing_public_subnet
```

```
aws_subnet.publishing_private_subnet
aws_iam_role.publishing_backend_role
aws_iam_instance_profile.publishing_backend_profile
# ... other imported resources ...
```

Here, the **state list** command displays all resources currently tracked in OpenTofu's state.

Inspect Specific Resources

To ensure that each imported resource's attributes in the state file match the actual configurations in AWS, use the **opentofu show** command.

For example, let us say that we are inspecting the EC2 Instance as below:

```
opentofu show aws_instance.publishing_backend_prod
```

Given below is the expected output:

```
{
  "id": "i-0abcd1234efgh5678",
  "ami": "ami-0abcdef1234567890",
  "instance_type": "t3.large",
  "subnet_id": "subnet-0abcd1234efgh5678",
  "security_groups": ["sg-0123abcd4567efgh8"],
  "iam_instance_profile": "publishing-backend-profile",
  "tags": {
    "Name": "publishing-backend-prod"
  },
  // ... other attributes ...
}
```

Here, the **show** command displays detailed information about a specific resource. And try to confirm that attributes like **ami**, **instance_type**, and **subnet_id** accurately reflect the actual settings in AWS. Post this, you need to prevent OpenTofu from attempting to modify resources during future **apply** operations., This you can do by ensuring that your **.tf** configuration files accurately represent the imported resources' current state.

Validate and Format Configuration files

After updating your configuration files, make sure they are properly formatted and free of syntax errors.

For example:

```
opentofu fmt
opentofu validate
```

Given below is the expected output:

```
Success! The configuration is valid.
```

Final Plan to Confirm State Alignment

Next, execute a **plan** to verify that OpenTofu recognizes the updated configurations and that no further changes are required.

For example:

```
opentofu plan -var-file=prod.tfvars
```

Given below is the expected output:

```
No changes. Infrastructure is up-to-date.
```

If the **plan** indicates no changes, the state file is already up-to-date, and no further action is needed. However, if there are minor adjustments required, apply the changes to finalize the state as shown below:

```
opentofu apply -var-file=prod.tfvars
```

Commit Updated Configuration and State files

Once reconciliation is complete and the state file is accurate, commit your updated configuration files to version control as below.

```
git add main.tf variables.tf prod.tfvars
git commit -m "Reconcile imported resources: Update EC2 and RDS configurations"
git push origin main
```

After importing resources, you must update and finalize the state file. This is a crucial step in integrating existing infrastructure into OpenTofu's management. To ensure accurate representation and management of your infrastructure, you must meticulously review imported resources, align your configuration files with actual resource attributes, and validate the state file.

Summary

This chapter provided a clear, step-by-step approach for integrating pre-existing resources into OpenTofu's state management. The chapter began by showing how to identify which infrastructure components were suitable for import, using a publishing application as a practical example. It emphasized conducting a thorough inventory of existing resources, assessing their compatibility, and understanding dependencies to ensure a smooth import process. The import command section thoroughly explained its syntax and usage, demonstrating how to associate unmanaged AWS resources such as EC2 instances and RDS databases with OpenTofu's state. The chapter then took you through practical steps to define resources in configuration files, execute import commands, and verify successful integration. This ensured that OpenTofu could effectively manage these resources moving forward.

The chapter also covered post-import reconciliation and updating the state file. You learned how to identify and resolve configuration mismatches between OpenTofu configurations and the actual infrastructure to ensure alignment and prevent unintended changes. You covered techniques such as updating .tf files with actual resource attributes, using lifecycle blocks to manage unmanaged attributes, and validating configurations with the opentofu plan command. By following these instructions, you can ensure that your imported infrastructure remains consistent, secure, and efficiently managed within OpenTofu, enabling seamless infrastructure as code practices.

CHAPTER 10: DEPLOYING AND SCALING INFRASTRUCTURE

Introduction

This chapter will teach you the essential processes and best practices for effectively deploying and managing your infrastructure using OpenTofu. This chapter will take you through the entire lifecycle of infrastructure deployment, ensuring that your applications are successfully launched and remain robust and scalable as demands evolve.

The chapter begins with Staging and Testing Deployments, where you will learn how to create controlled environments to validate infrastructure changes before they impact live systems. This section emphasizes the importance of thorough testing to identify and resolve potential issues early, reducing the risk of downtime and ensuring that your deployments meet quality standards. You will gain practical insights into setting up staging environments, implementing automated tests, and utilizing OpenTofu's features to streamline the deployment pipeline.

Next, the chapter moves on to Promoting Changes to Production, where you will learn how to safely and efficiently move validated changes from staging to your production environment. You will discover techniques for minimizing disruptions, managing version control, and implementing rollback plans to handle unforeseen issues. Finally, you will learn both vertical and horizontal scaling methods, leveraging OpenTofu's automation capabilities to dynamically adjust resources.

Staging and Testing Deployments

A staging environment mirrors the production setup as closely as possible, allowing you to validate changes, perform thorough testing, and ensure that new deployments won't disrupt your live application. We will walk through the practical steps to deploy the infrastructure of our publishing application to a staging environment using OpenTofu. This process involves setting up a dedicated workspace, configuring environment-specific variables, deploying resources, and conducting validation tests to ensure everything operates seamlessly before promoting changes to production.

Deploying Infrastructure to Staging

With the staging workspace and variables configured, learned in the previous chapters, we can now directly proceed to deploy the infrastructure.

We can follow the below steps:

- Initialize the OpenTofu and validate the configuration

```
opentofu init
opentofu validate
```

- Plan the deployment

```
opentofu plan -var-file=staging.tfvars
```

This generates an execution plan, showing what actions OpenTofu will take to deploy the infrastructure. Review this plan to ensure that the changes align with your expectations.

- Next, apply the deployment

```
opentofu apply -var-file=staging.tfvars
```

- List the resources in state

```
opentofu state list
```

Given below is the expected output:

```
aws_instance.publishing_backend_staging
aws_db_instance.publishing_db_staging
aws_security_group.publishing_backend_sg_staging
aws_security_group.publishing_db_sg_staging
aws_vpc.publishing_vpc_staging
aws_subnet.publishing_public_subnet_staging
aws_subnet.publishing_private_subnet_staging
aws_iam_role.publishing_backend_role_staging
aws_iam_instance_profile.publishing_backend_profile_staging
# ... other resources ...
```

- And finally, inspect the specific resources

```
opentofu show aws_instance.publishing_backend_staging
opentofu show aws_db_instance.publishing_db_staging
```

We here use the **show** command to inspect the details of specific resources, ensuring that all attributes are correctly configured.

Conducting Validation and Testing

When we deploy to staging, it's not just about getting things set up. It's about making sure the infrastructure is running how it should. You've got to run thorough validation and testing to find and fix any issues before you can promote changes to production.

Below is an example of running the integration tests:

```
# Assuming you have a script or tool for integration tests
./scripts/run_integration_tests.sh
```

This executes a suite of tests that interact with the staging environment, validating connectivity, performance, and functionality.

We also need to setup the monitoring and logging to track the health and performance of your staging environment.

For example, we are integrating the CloudWatch as shown below:

```
resource "aws_cloudwatch_log_group"
"publishing_backend_logs_staging" {
  name              = "/aws/ecs/publishing-backend-staging"
  retention_in_days = 14
}
resource "aws_cloudwatch_log_stream"
"publishing_backend_stream_staging" {
  name           = "publishing-backend-stream-staging"
  log_group_name =
aws_cloudwatch_log_group.publishing_backend_logs_staging.name
}
```

This creates CloudWatch log groups and streams to collect and monitor logs from your application instances.

Apart from this, we can also conduct security assessments to ensure that your staging environment adheres to best practices. We can simply run the AWS trusted advisor checks:

```
aws support describe-trusted-advisor-checks
aws support describe-trusted-advisor-check-result --check-id
<check-id> --language en
```

Feedback-based Iteration

After deploying and testing your staging environment, gather feedback and make necessary adjustments. This is done by reviewing the outcomes of your automated and manual tests to identify any issues or areas for improvement.

For example, adjusting instance types for better performance

```
# staging.tfvars
instance_type = "t3.large"  # Increased from t3.medium based on performance tests
```

Next, we then apply the updated configurations to the staging environment to implement the changes.

```
opentofu apply -var-file=staging.tfvars
```

Keep repeating the validation and testing steps, just to ensure that the changes have resolved the identified issues and that the environment remains stable.

Prepare Promotion to Production

Once the staging environment is validated and stable, you can prepare to promote the changes to the production environment. Now to do this, we need to maintain clear documentation of the changes made during the staging phase, including configuration updates and test results. And also, we need to ensure that the production workspace has the necessary configurations and that no staging-specific settings are inadvertently applied to production.

Implement Version Control

We can simply use Git to track changes, enabling rollback if necessary.

```
git add .
git commit -m "Deploy infrastructure to staging environment for validation"
git push origin staging
```

Setup CI/CD

Next, Integrate OpenTofu deployments into your CI/CD pipeline to automate the promotion of changes from staging to production. Following is the GitHub Actions Workflow code:

```
name: Deploy to Staging
on:
  push:
    branches:
      - develop
```

```
jobs:
  deploy-staging:
    runs-on: ubuntu-latest
    steps:
      - name: Checkout Code
        uses: actions/checkout@v2
      - name: Set up OpenTofu
        uses: hashicorp/setup-opentofu@v1
        with:
          opentofu_version: "latest"
      - name: Configure AWS Credentials
        uses: aws-actions/configure-aws-credentials@v1
        with:
          aws-access-key-id: ${{ secrets.AWS_ACCESS_KEY_ID }}
          aws-secret-access-key: ${{
secrets.AWS_SECRET_ACCESS_KEY }}
          aws-region: us-east-1
      - name: Initialize OpenTofu
        run: opentofu init
      - name: Select Staging Workspace
        run: opentofu workspace select staging
      - name: Validate Configuration
        run: opentofu validate
      - name: Plan Deployment
        run: opentofu plan -var-file=staging.tfvars -
out=staging.plan
      - name: Apply Deployment
        run: opentofu apply staging.plan
```

This above program automates the deployment of infrastructure changes to the staging environment upon pushes to the develop branch.

Promoting Changes to Production

After successfully deploying and validating your infrastructure in the staging environment, the next task is **promoting these changes to the production environment**. Promoting changes involves replicating the validated configurations from staging to production, maintaining consistency, minimizing downtime, and ensuring that the production environment remains stable and secure.

Preparing the Production Workspace

Before promoting changes, first we must make sure that the production workspace is properly set up and isolated from staging to prevent unintended interactions.

Create a Production Workspace

```
opentofu workspace new prod
```

This command creates a new workspace named **`prod`**. If it already exists, OpenTofu will notify you.

Select the Production Workspace

```
opentofu workspace select prod
```

This switches the current working environment to prod, ensuring that all subsequent commands affect the production workspace.

Ensuring Configuration Consistency

To promote changes, your production configurations should mirror those of staging, with environment-specific adjustments as necessary. This involves ensuring that your **`.tf`** files and variable files (**`.tfvars`**) are correctly set up for production.

Review and Update Variable Files

Create or update the production variable file (**`prod.tfvars`**) to reflect production-specific settings.

```
# prod.tfvars
environment       = "prod"
instance_type     = "t3.large"
db_instance_class = "db.t3.large"
```

```
ami_id               = "ami-0abcdef1234567890"  # Replace with a
valid production AMI
allowed_ssh_cidrs = ["198.51.100.0/24"]
db_password          = "ProdSecurePass123!"
enable_load_balancer = true
enable_advanced_analytics = true
```

Update the Configuration files

We need to check that our production configurations are correctly defined, reflecting any necessary differences from staging.

```
# main.tf
provider "aws" {
  region = "us-east-1"
}
resource "aws_vpc" "publishing_vpc" {
  cidr_block              = "10.0.0.0/16"
  enable_dns_support    = true
  enable_dns_hostnames = true
  tags = {
    Name = "publishing-vpc-prod"
  }
}
resource "aws_subnet" "publishing_public_subnet" {
  vpc_id                = aws_vpc.publishing_vpc.id
  cidr_block            = "10.0.1.0/24"
  availability_zone = "us-east-1a"
  tags = {
    Name = "publishing-public-subnet-prod"
  }
}
```

```
resource "aws_subnet" "publishing_private_subnet" {
  vpc_id                  = aws_vpc.publishing_vpc.id
  cidr_block              = "10.0.2.0/24"
  availability_zone = "us-east-1a"
  tags = {
    Name = "publishing-private-subnet-prod"
  }
}
resource "aws_security_group" "publishing_backend_sg" {
  name        = "publishing-backend-sg-prod"
  description = "Security group for Publishing Backend in
Prod"
  vpc_id      = aws_vpc.publishing_vpc.id
  ingress {
    from_port   = 22
    to_port     = 22
    protocol    = "tcp"
    cidr_blocks = var.allowed_ssh_cidrs
  }
  ingress {
    from_port   = 80
    to_port     = 80
    protocol    = "tcp"
    cidr_blocks = ["0.0.0.0/0"]
  }
  ingress {
    from_port   = 443
    to_port     = 443
    protocol    = "tcp"
```

```
    cidr_blocks = ["0.0.0.0/0"]
  }
  egress {
    from_port   = 0
    to_port     = 0
    protocol    = "-1"
    cidr_blocks = ["0.0.0.0/0"]
  }
  tags = {
    Name = "publishing-backend-sg-prod"
  }
}
resource "aws_instance" "publishing_backend_prod" {
  ami           = var.ami_id
  instance_type = var.instance_type
  subnet_id     = aws_subnet.publishing_public_subnet.id
  security_groups =
[aws_security_group.publishing_backend_sg.name]
  iam_instance_profile =
aws_iam_instance_profile.publishing_backend_profile.name
  tags = {
    Name = "publishing-backend-prod"
  }
  lifecycle {
    ignore_changes = [
      associate_public_ip_address,
    ]
  }
}
resource "aws_db_instance" "publishing_db_prod" {
```

```
  identifier                = "publishing-db-prod"
  engine                    = "postgres"
  engine_version            = "13.3"
  instance_class            = var.db_instance_class
  allocated_storage         = 200
  storage_type              = "gp2"
  name                      = "publishingdb-prod"
  username                  = "prod_admin"
  password                  = var.db_password
  parameter_group_name      = "default.postgres13"
  skip_final_snapshot       = true
  publicly_accessible       = false
  vpc_security_group_ids    =
[aws_security_group.publishing_db_sg.id]
  db_subnet_group_name      =
aws_db_subnet_group.publishing_db_subnet_group.name
  multi_az                  = false
  auto_minor_version_upgrade = true
  tags = {
    Name = "publishing-db-prod"
  }
  lifecycle {
    ignore_changes = [
      backup_retention_period,
    ]
  }
}
```

We can also define the other necessary resources like IAM roles, instance profiles, load balancers, etc. at this stage itself.

Applying Configuration to Production

Once the above plan is ready, we can simply proceed to apply the changes to the production environment, but cautiously with below steps.

- Apply the changes

```
opentofu apply -var-file=prod.tfvars
```

You can expect the below output:

```
aws_instance.publishing_backend_prod: Modifying... [id=i-0abcd1234efgh5678]
aws_db_instance.publishing_db_prod: Modifying...
[id=publishing-db-prod]
...
Apply complete! Resources: X added, Y changed, Z destroyed.
```

- Verify the deployment

After the apply operation completes, verify that all resources are correctly deployed and functioning as expected.

- List the resources in production state

```
opentofu state list
```

- Inspect the specific resources

```
opentofu show aws_instance.publishing_backend_prod
opentofu show aws_db_instance.publishing_db_prod
```

Implementing Rollback Plans

There are cases and scenarios when unforeseen issues may arise during or after promotion to production. Having a rollback plan ensures that you can quickly revert to a stable state to minimize downtime and impact on users.

So, we will track the configuration changes in Git to facilitate easy rollback if needed

```
git add .
git commit -m "Promote staging configurations to production"
```

```
git push origin prod
```

For critical resources like databases, we create snapshots before applying significant changes as shown below.

```
aws rds create-db-snapshot --db-instance-identifier
publishing-db-prod --db-snapshot-identifier publishing-db-
prod-snapshot-$(date +%F)
```

This creates a snapshot of the RDS instance, allowing you to restore it in case of issues.

We then develop scripts to automate the rollback process, ensuring a swift response to production issues.

Following is a sample Rollback program:

```
#!/bin/bash

# Select the production workspace

opentofu workspace select prod

# Revert to the previous Git commit

git reset --hard HEAD~1

# Apply the reverted configuration

opentofu apply -auto-approve -var-file=prod.tfvars
```

This reverts the last commit in Git and applies the previous configuration to OpenTofu, effectively rolling back the infrastructure changes.

By following all these steps—preparing the production workspace, ensuring configuration consistency, deploying and validating resources, and implementing rollback plans—you establish a robust and secure promotion process using OpenTofu.

Scaling Infrastructure

As your publishing application grows and user demands increase, it becomes essential to **scale your infrastructure** to maintain performance, reliability, and availability. Scaling ensures that your application can handle varying loads without compromising user experience. OpenTofu facilitates dynamic scaling through configurations that allow your infrastructure to adjust automatically based on real-time metrics and predefined thresholds. We will learn to add capacity dynamically to our already deployed publishing application using OpenTofu. This includes setting up Auto Scaling Groups (ASGs) for EC2 instances, configuring scaling policies, and ensuring that other resources like load balancers and databases are optimized for scalability.

Figuring-out Scaling Requirements

Before you implement scaling, you need to understand the specific scaling requirements of your application. First, identify the key metrics that influence performance and resource needs.Monitor CPU utilization, as high CPU usage can signal the need for additional instances.Analyze memory usage, as memory bottlenecks may negatively impact application performance. Evaluate network traffic, as increases in inbound or outbound data may require additional resources.Observe request rates, since higher rates can necessitate scaling up to maintain optimal response times.

Then, you need to figure out the best scaling policies. Think about scaling out, which means adding instances to handle higher demand. Plan for scaling in, which removes instances during slower periods. Use scheduled scaling to prepare for predictable traffic patterns, like peak usage hours. Finally, set the desired capacity by defining the minimum, maximum, and desired number of instances in your Auto Scaling Group. This configuration makes sure that scaling matches your application's needs and adapts to changes in demand effectively.

OpenTofu Configuration for Auto Scaling

To enable dynamic scaling, update your OpenTofu configuration files to include an Auto Scaling Group (ASG) and associated policies.

Define Launch Configuration

A Launch Configuration or Launch Template specifies the configuration for the EC2 instances that the ASG will manage.

Given below is the sample launch template:

```
resource "aws_launch_template" "publishing_backend_lt" {
  name_prefix   = "publishing-backend-"
  image_id      = var.ami_id
  instance_type = var.instance_type

  iam_instance_profile {
    name =
aws_iam_instance_profile.publishing_backend_profile.name
  }

  network_interfaces {
```

```
    associate_public_ip_address = false
    subnet_id                   =
aws_subnet.publishing_public_subnet.id
    security_groups             =
[aws_security_group.publishing_backend_sg.id]
  }

  tag_specifications {
    resource_type = "instance"
    tags = {
      Name        = "publishing-backend-prod"
      Environment = var.environment
    }
  }

  lifecycle {
    create_before_destroy = true
  }
}
```

In the above, the Launch Template defines the AMI, instance type, IAM role, network settings, and tags for EC2 instances. And the Lifecycle ensures that a new launch template is created before destroying the old one, preventing downtime.

Create Auto Scaling Group

The ASG manages the number of EC2 instances based on scaling policies. Given below is the Auto Scaling Group created:

```
resource "aws_autoscaling_group" "publishing_backend_asg" {
  launch_template {
    id      = aws_launch_template.publishing_backend_lt.id
    version = "$Latest"
  }
```

```
  vpc_zone_identifier = [
    aws_subnet.publishing_public_subnet.id,
    aws_subnet.publishing_private_subnet.id
  ]

  min_size = 2
  max_size = 10
  desired_capacity = 3

  target_group_arns =
[aws_lb_target_group.publishing_lb_tg_prod.arn]

  tag {
    key                 = "Name"
    value               = "publishing-backend-prod"
    propagate_at_launch = true
  }

  lifecycle {
    create_before_destroy = true
  }

  # Enable scaling based on metrics
  enabled_metrics = ["GroupDesiredCapacity",
"GroupInServiceInstances", "GroupMaxSize", "GroupMinSize"]
}
```

Configure Scaling Policies

We then define the scaling policies that dictate when and how the ASG should scale.

```
resource "aws_autoscaling_policy" "scale_out" {
  name                   = "scale-out-policy"
  autoscaling_group_name =
aws_autoscaling_group.publishing_backend_asg.name
  policy_type            = "SimpleScaling"
  adjustment_type        = "ChangeInCapacity"
  scaling_adjustment     = 1
  cooldown               = 300
}

resource "aws_autoscaling_policy" "scale_in" {
  name                   = "scale-in-policy"
  autoscaling_group_name =
aws_autoscaling_group.publishing_backend_asg.name
  policy_type            = "SimpleScaling"
  adjustment_type        = "ChangeInCapacity"
  scaling_adjustment     = -1
  cooldown               = 300
}

resource "aws_cloudwatch_metric_alarm" "high_cpu_alarm" {
  alarm_name          = "high_cpu_alarm"
  comparison_operator = "GreaterThanThreshold"
  evaluation_periods  = "2"
  metric_name         = "CPUUtilization"
  namespace           = "AWS/EC2"
  period              = "300"
  statistic           = "Average"
  threshold           = "70"
  alarm_description   = "Alarm when CPU exceeds 70%"
```

```
  dimensions = {
    AutoScalingGroupName =
aws_autoscaling_group.publishing_backend_asg.name
  }

  alarm_actions = [aws_autoscaling_policy.scale_out.arn]
  ok_actions    = [aws_autoscaling_policy.scale_in.arn]
}

resource "aws_cloudwatch_metric_alarm" "low_cpu_alarm" {
  alarm_name          = "low_cpu_alarm"
  comparison_operator = "LessThanThreshold"
  evaluation_periods  = "2"
  metric_name         = "CPUUtilization"
  namespace           = "AWS/EC2"
  period              = "300"
  statistic           = "Average"
  threshold           = "30"
  alarm_description   = "Alarm when CPU is below 30%"
  dimensions = {
    AutoScalingGroupName =
aws_autoscaling_group.publishing_backend_asg.name
  }

  alarm_actions = [aws_autoscaling_policy.scale_in.arn]
  ok_actions    = [aws_autoscaling_policy.scale_out.arn]
}
```

In the above policy script,

- Scale-Out Policy increases the ASG capacity by one instance when CPU utilization exceeds 70%.

- Scale-In Policy decreases the ASG capacity by one instance when CPU utilization drops below 30%.
- CloudWatch Alarms monitors CPU utilization and triggers the appropriate scaling policies based on thresholds.

Applying Scaling Configuration

With the Auto Scaling configurations defined, apply the changes to update your infrastructure. For this, you need to validate the configuration, plan the deployment and then we directly apply the configuration.

```
opentofu init
opentofu validate
opentofu plan -var-file=prod.tfvars
  # aws_launch_template.publishing_backend_lt will be created
  + resource "aws_launch_template" "publishing_backend_lt" {
      + ami                               = "ami-0abcdef1234567890"
      + instance_type                     = "t3.large"
      + name_prefix                       = "publishing-backend-"
      + ...
    }
  # aws_autoscaling_group.publishing_backend_asg will be
created
  + resource "aws_autoscaling_group" "publishing_backend_asg"
{
      + desired_capacity                  = 3
      + max_size                          = 10
      + min_size                          = 2
      + ...
    }
  # aws_autoscaling_policy.scale_out will be created
  + resource "aws_autoscaling_policy" "scale_out" {
      + adjustment_type                   = "ChangeInCapacity"
```

```
      + autoscaling_group_name         = "publishing-backend-
asg"
      + scaling_adjustment             = 1
      + ...
    }
  # aws_autoscaling_policy.scale_in will be created
  + resource "aws_autoscaling_policy" "scale_in" {
      + adjustment_type                = "ChangeInCapacity"
      + autoscaling_group_name         = "publishing-backend-
asg"
      + scaling_adjustment             = -1
      + ...
    }
  # aws_cloudwatch_metric_alarm.high_cpu_alarm will be created
  + resource "aws_cloudwatch_metric_alarm" "high_cpu_alarm" {
      + alarm_actions                  =
["arn:aws:autoscaling:...:policy/scale-out-policy"]
      + comparison_operator            = "GreaterThanThreshold"
      + metric_name                    = "CPUUtilization"
      + namespace                      = "AWS/EC2"
      + ...
    }
  # aws_cloudwatch_metric_alarm.low_cpu_alarm will be created
  + resource "aws_cloudwatch_metric_alarm" "low_cpu_alarm" {
      + alarm_actions                  =
["arn:aws:autoscaling:...:policy/scale-in-policy"]
      + comparison_operator            = "LessThanThreshold"
      + metric_name                    = "CPUUtilization"
      + namespace                      = "AWS/EC2"
      + ...
```

```
    }
  # Additional resources to be created...
opentofu apply -var-file=prod.tfvars
```

This above script will execute the planned actions to create the launch template, Auto Scaling Group, scaling policies, and CloudWatch alarms. The OpenTofu will prompt for confirmation. You just review the changes and confirm to proceed.

Following will be the sample output:

```
aws_launch_template.publishing_backend_lt: Creating...
aws_launch_template.publishing_backend_lt: Creation complete after Xs [id=lt-0abcd1234efgh5678]
aws_autoscaling_group.publishing_backend_asg: Creating...
aws_autoscaling_group.publishing_backend_asg: Creation complete after Ys [id=publishing-backend-asg]
aws_autoscaling_policy.scale_out: Creating...
aws_autoscaling_policy.scale_out: Creation complete after Zs [id=scale-out-policy]
aws_autoscaling_policy.scale_in: Creating...
aws_autoscaling_policy.scale_in: Creation complete after Ws [id=scale-in-policy]
aws_cloudwatch_metric_alarm.high_cpu_alarm: Creating...
aws_cloudwatch_metric_alarm.high_cpu_alarm: Creation complete after Es [id=high_cpu_alarm]
aws_cloudwatch_metric_alarm.low_cpu_alarm: Creating...
aws_cloudwatch_metric_alarm.low_cpu_alarm: Creation complete after Rs [id=low_cpu_alarm]
Apply complete! Resources: X added, Y changed, Z destroyed.
```

Verifying Auto Scaling Configuration

Once you've got the scaling set up, double-check that the Auto Scaling Group and the scaling policies are working like they should.

- List Auto Scaling Groups

```
opentofu state list | grep aws_autoscaling_group
```

- Inspect the Auto Scaling Group

```
opentofu show aws_autoscaling_group.publishing_backend_asg
```

You may get the following output


```
{
  "id": "publishing-backend-asg",
  "launch_template": {
    "id": "lt-0abcd1234efgh5678",
    "version": "$Latest"
  },
  "min_size": 2,
  "max_size": 10,
  "desired_capacity": 3,
  "target_group_arns": [
    "arn:aws:elasticloadbalancing:us-east-
1:123456789012:targetgroup/publishing-lb-tg-
prod/abcd1234efgh5678"
  ],
  "tags": [
    {
      "key": "Name",
      "value": "publishing-backend-prod",
      "propagate_at_launch": true
    }
  ],
  // ... other attributes ...
}
```


- Check CloudWatch Alarms

```
opentofu show aws_cloudwatch_metric_alarm.high_cpu_alarm
opentofu show aws_cloudwatch_metric_alarm.low_cpu_alarm
```

Cost Management and Optimization

Dynamic scaling can cause your costs to go up and down. So, it's important to implement strategies to manage and optimize your infrastructure costs effectively.

Use Spot Instances

You can use them in your ASG, especially for workloads that aren't mission-critical. Following is how to set up Spot Instances in a Launch Template:

```
resource "aws_launch_template" "publishing_backend_lt" {
  ...
  instance_market_options {
    market_type = "spot"
    spot_options {
      max_price = "0.05"  # Maximum price you are willing to
pay per hour
    }
  }
  ...
}
```

You can use spare AWS capacity at discounted rates. Just set a cap on the price per hour to control costs.

Resource Tagging

Tag your resources so you can track and allocate costs accurately across different teams or projects. Following is an example of adding cost allocation tags:

```
resource "aws_instance" "publishing_backend_prod" {
  ...
  tags = {
    Name        = "publishing-backend-prod"
```

```
    Environment = var.environment
    Project     = "PublishingApp"
    CostCenter  = "12345"
  }
  ...
}
```

It's crucial to keep up the performance and reliability of your publishing app as user demand changes by scaling your infrastructure in real time.

Summary

In short, you learned the key strategies and hands-on steps to use OpenTofu for your infrastructure. You explored setting up a dedicated staging workspace that mirrored your production environment. You got the hang of environment-specific configurations, automated and manual testing, and thorough validation to make sure infrastructure changes functioned correctly before impacting live users. And by testing everything out in a staging environment, you caught and fixed any potential problems before they affected actual users, making your app more reliable and stable.

Then, you learned how to promote changes to production and scale the infrastructure. Promoting changes meant moving validated configurations from staging to production, making sure everything stayed consistent, minimizing downtime, and having solid rollback plans for anything that might go wrong. Then, we looked at how to scale up your infrastructure. You can do this by using something called Auto Scaling Groups (ASGs). You can also define scaling policies based on important things like CPU utilization. And you can set up CloudWatch alarms for automated scaling actions. By doing all this, you got a plan for setting up infrastructure that can adapt, is strong, and is managed well, so your application can grow smoothly as more and more people use it.

CHAPTER 11: ADVANCED FEATURES AND AUTOMATION

Introduction

This chapter is going to dive into how you can take your infrastructure management to the next level by using OpenTofu with some cool tools and techniques. You will learn how to take your IaC practices to the next level, streamline operations, boost security, and improve scalability.

It starts with Automating Infrastructure Updates, where you will learn to set up automated processes for applying configuration changes, keeping things consistent, and avoiding human error. Then, we will dive into Dynamic Resource Creation, where you will learn how to provision resources on-demand based on real-time needs and predefined conditions. Then, you will dive into Managing Secrets in Configurations, where you will learn how to integrate secret management solutions. This'll help keep your configurations secure and in line with industry standards. And finally, Integrating Third-Party Tools will show you how to connect OpenTofu with other services to automate workflows, improve teamwork, and set up CI/CD pipelines.

Automating Infrastructure Updates

Overview

Automating infrastructure updates is a cornerstone of modern DevOps practices, enabling teams to deploy changes rapidly, consistently, and reliably. By integrating OpenTofu with CI/CD pipelines, you can streamline the process of applying infrastructure changes, reduce manual interventions, and minimize the risk of human error. This section will take you through the practical steps of setting up automated deployments using OpenTofu in a CI/CD pipeline, with a focus on leveraging GitHub Actions as the automation tool. Using our publishing application as an example, you will learn how to create a seamless workflow that automatically applies infrastructure changes whenever code is pushed to your repository.

Automating infrastructure updates offers numerous advantages:

1. Automation ensures that infrastructure is provisioned in a consistent manner across different environments, eliminating discrepancies caused by manual configurations.
2. Automated pipelines can deploy changes much faster than manual processes, accelerating the development lifecycle and enabling rapid iterations.
3. By minimizing manual interventions, automation decreases the likelihood of configuration errors and misdeployments.
4. CI/CD pipelines facilitate better collaboration among team members by providing a clear and auditable process for deploying changes.
5. Automation supports scaling infrastructure seamlessly to meet increasing demands without additional manual effort.

Setting up a CI/CD Pipeline

To automate infrastructure updates with OpenTofu, you need to integrate it into your CI/CD pipeline. Here, we will set up automated deployments. Let's walk through setting up a GitHub Actions workflow to automate OpenTofu deployments for our publishing application.

Storing Secrets in GitHub

First, store your AWS credentials and any other sensitive variables as GitHub Secrets to ensure they are securely managed. You may follow the following steps:

- Go to your GitHub repository.
- Click on **`Settings`** > **`Secrets and variables`** > **`Actions`**.
- Click on **`New repository secret`**.
- Add the following secrets:
    - **`AWS_ACCESS_KEY_ID`**: Your AWS access key ID.
    - **`AWS_SECRET_ACCESS_KEY`**: Your AWS secret access key.
    - **`TF_VAR_db_password`**: (Optional) Any sensitive variables required by your OpenTofu configuration.

Creating GitHub Actions Workflow

In your repository, create a directory named **`.github/workflows`** if it doesn't exist. Inside this directory, create a file named **`deploy.yml`**.

```
mkdir -p .github/workflows
touch .github/workflows/deploy.yml
```

Next, open **`deploy.yml`** and add the following content:

```
name: OpenTofu Deployment
on:
  push:
    branches:
      - main
      - staging
jobs:
```

```
  deploy:
    runs-on: ubuntu-latest
    steps:
      - name: Checkout Repository
        uses: actions/checkout@v3
      - name: Set up OpenTofu
        uses: hashicorp/setup-opentofu@v1
        with:
          opentofu_version: "latest"
      - name: Configure AWS Credentials
        uses: aws-actions/configure-aws-credentials@v1
        with:
          aws-access-key-id: ${{ secrets.AWS_ACCESS_KEY_ID }}
          aws-secret-access-key: ${{
secrets.AWS_SECRET_ACCESS_KEY }}
          aws-region: us-east-1
      - name: Initialize OpenTofu
        run: opentofu init
      - name: Validate OpenTofu Configuration
        run: opentofu validate
      - name: Plan Infrastructure Changes
        id: plan
        run: opentofu plan -var-file=vars/${{ github.ref ==
'refs/heads/main' && 'prod.tfvars' || 'staging.tfvars'
}}.tfvars -out=plan.out
      - name: Upload Plan for Review
        if: github.ref == 'refs/heads/main'
        uses: actions/upload-artifact@v3
        with:
          name: opentofu-plan
```

```
      path: plan.out
  - name: Apply Infrastructure Changes
    if: github.ref == 'refs/heads/main'
    run: opentofu apply -auto-approve plan.out
  - name: Apply Infrastructure Changes to Staging
    if: github.ref == 'refs/heads/staging'
    run: opentofu apply -auto-approve plan.out
  - name: Notify Success
    if: success()
    uses: actions/github-script@v6
    with:
      script: |
        github.issues.createComment({
          issue_number: 1,
          owner: context.repo.owner,
          repo: context.repo.repo,
          body: "OpenTofu deployment succeeded!"
        })
```

Committing and Pushing the Workflow

After defining the workflow, commit and push it to your repository.

```
git add .github/workflows/deploy.yml
git commit -m "Add GitHub Actions workflow for OpenTofu
deployments"
git push origin main
```

Testing the Automated Deployment

To ensure that the automated deployment works as intended, we now perform a test deployment.

For this, first modify a configuration in the staging environment and push it to the **staging** branch.

```
git checkout staging
# Make changes to staging configurations
git add .
git commit -m "Update staging configurations for testing"
git push origin staging
```

Next, after validating changes in staging, merge them into the **main** branch to promote them to production.

```
git checkout main
git merge staging
git push origin main
```

This merge triggers the GitHub Actions workflow to apply the changes to the production environment automatically.

By following the above steps, we can establish a resilient and efficient infrastructure deployment process.

Managing Secrets in Configurations

Secrets such as API keys, database passwords, and certificates are critical to the security and integrity of your applications. Mishandling these sensitive data can lead to unauthorized access, data breaches, and compromised systems. We will explore strategies for managing secrets within OpenTofu configurations, ensuring that your sensitive information remains protected throughout your deployment workflows. Using our publishing application as an example, you will learn how to integrate secure secret management practices into your OpenTofu workflows, leveraging tools like environment variables, GitHub Secrets, and dedicated secret management services.

Best Practices for Managing Secrets

Before diving into practical implementations, it's essential to understand the best practices for managing secrets:

1. Never embed secrets directly within your configuration files. This practice exposes sensitive information to anyone with access to the codebase.
2. Store secrets in environment variables to decouple sensitive data from your code.
3. Utilize dedicated secret management tools like AWS Secrets Manager, HashiCorp Vault, or Azure Key Vault for enhanced security and management capabilities.

4. Ensure that your OpenTofu state files, which may contain sensitive information, are encrypted and stored securely.
5. Restrict access to secrets to only those individuals and services that require them, following the principle of least privilege.
6. Implement secret rotation policies to minimize the risk of compromised credentials.

Strategies for Managing Secrets

Let's explore several practical methods to manage secrets securely within OpenTofu configurations.

Using Sensitive Variables

OpenTofu allows you to mark variables as sensitive, preventing them from being displayed in logs or state files.

- Define Sensitive Variables

In your **variables.tf**, mark sensitive variables appropriately.

```
# variables.tf
variable "db_password" {
  description = "Database admin password"
  type        = string
  sensitive   = true
}
variable "api_key" {
  description = "API key for external service"
  type        = string
  sensitive   = true
}
```

- Reference Sensitive Variables Securely

In your configuration files, reference these variables without exposing their values.

```
# main.tf
resource "aws_db_instance" "publishing_db_prod" {
  identifier                  = "publishing-db-prod"
```

```
  engine                    = "postgres"
  engine_version            = "13.3"
  instance_class            = "db.t3.large"
  allocated_storage         = 200
  storage_type              = "gp2"
  name                      = "publishingdb-prod"
  username                  = "prod_admin"
  password                  = var.db_password
  parameter_group_name      = "default.postgres13"
  skip_final_snapshot       = true
  publicly_accessible       = false
  vpc_security_group_ids    =
[aws_security_group.publishing_db_sg.id]
  db_subnet_group_name      =
aws_db_subnet_group.publishing_db_subnet_group.name
  multi_az                  = false
  auto_minor_version_upgrade = true
  tags = {
    Name = "publishing-db-prod"
  }
  lifecycle {
    ignore_changes = [
      backup_retention_period,
    ]
  }
}
resource "aws_instance" "publishing_backend_prod" {
  ami           = var.ami_id
  instance_type = var.instance_type
  subnet_id     = aws_subnet.publishing_public_subnet.id
```

```
  security_groups =
[aws_security_group.publishing_backend_sg.name]
  iam_instance_profile =
aws_iam_instance_profile.publishing_backend_profile.name
  user_data = <<-EOF
              #!/bin/bash
              export API_KEY=${var.api_key}
              EOF
  tags = {
    Name        = "publishing-backend-prod"
    Environment = "production"
  }
  lifecycle {
    ignore_changes = [
      associate_public_ip_address,
    ]
  }
}
```

In the above, the **db_password** and **api_key** variables are marked as sensitive, ensuring they are not exposed in logs or state outputs. And, the **api_key** is injected securely into the EC2 instance's environment without exposing it in the configuration.

Integrating with Secret Management Services

Using dedicated secret management services enhances the security and management of your secrets. Here, we will use AWS Secrets Manager as an example.

- Store Secrets in AWS Secrets Manager

Store your secrets in AWS Secrets Manager via the AWS Console or CLI.

```
aws secretsmanager create-secret --name publishing_db_password
--secret-string "ProdSecurePass123!"

aws secretsmanager create-secret --name external_api_key --
secret-string "APIKEY1234567890"
```

- Fetch Secrets in OpenTofu Configuration

Use the **aws_secretsmanager_secret** and **aws_secretsmanager_secret_version** resources to retrieve secrets.

```
# secrets.tf
resource "aws_secretsmanager_secret" "publishing_db_password"
{
  name        = "publishing_db_password"
  description = "Database password for publishing application"
}
resource "aws_secretsmanager_secret_version"
"publishing_db_password_version" {
  secret_id     =
aws_secretsmanager_secret.publishing_db_password.id
  secret_string = var.db_password
}
resource "aws_secretsmanager_secret" "external_api_key" {
  name        = "external_api_key"
  description = "API key for external service integration"
}
resource "aws_secretsmanager_secret_version"
"external_api_key_version" {
  secret_id     =
aws_secretsmanager_secret.external_api_key.id
  secret_string = var.api_key
}
```

- Access Secrets in Resources

Use data sources to retrieve secret values securely.

```
# main.tf
data "aws_secretsmanager_secret_version"
"publishing_db_password" {
```

```
  secret_id =
aws_secretsmanager_secret.publishing_db_password.id
}
data "aws_secretsmanager_secret_version" "external_api_key" {
  secret_id = aws_secretsmanager_secret.external_api_key.id
}
resource "aws_db_instance" "publishing_db_prod" {
  ...
  password =
data.aws_secretsmanager_secret_version.publishing_db_password.
secret_string
  ...
}
resource "aws_instance" "publishing_backend_prod" {
  ...
  user_data = <<-EOF
              #!/bin/bash
              export
API_KEY=${data.aws_secretsmanager_secret_version.external_api_
key.secret_string}
              EOF
  ...
}
```

In this, the secrets are stored securely in AWS Secrets Manager. The OpenTofu fetches secrets at runtime using data sources, ensuring they are not hardcoded or exposed in configurations.

Using GitHub Secrets with GitHub Actions

Here, we integrate GitHub Secrets to manage secrets within your CI/CD pipelines securely.

- Store Secrets in GitHub

Add your secrets to GitHub repository secrets. To do this, navigate to your repository on GitHub. Then, go to **Settings** > **Secrets and variables** > **Actions**. And then, add secrets like **DB_PASSWORD** and **API_KEY**.

- Reference Secrets in GitHub Actions Workflow

Modify your GitHub Actions workflow to pass secrets as environment variables or OpenTofu variables.

```
# .github/workflows/deploy.yml
name: OpenTofu Deployment
on:
  push:
    branches:
      - main
      - staging
jobs:
  deploy:
    runs-on: ubuntu-latest
    steps:
      - name: Checkout Repository
        uses: actions/checkout@v3
      - name: Set up OpenTofu
        uses: hashicorp/setup-opentofu@v1
        with:
          opentofu_version: "latest"
      - name: Configure AWS Credentials
        uses: aws-actions/configure-aws-credentials@v1
        with:
          aws-access-key-id: ${{ secrets.AWS_ACCESS_KEY_ID }}
          aws-secret-access-key: ${{
secrets.AWS_SECRET_ACCESS_KEY }}
          aws-region: us-east-1
      - name: Initialize OpenTofu
        run: opentofu init
      - name: Validate OpenTofu Configuration
```

```
        run: opentofu validate
      - name: Plan Infrastructure Changes
        id: plan
        run: |
          opentofu plan \
            -var-file=vars/${{ github.ref == 'refs/heads/main'
&& 'prod.tfvars' || 'staging.tfvars' }}.tfvars \
            -var db_password=${{ secrets.DB_PASSWORD }} \
            -var api_key=${{ secrets.API_KEY }} \
            -out=plan.out
      - name: Apply Infrastructure Changes
        run: opentofu apply -auto-approve plan.out
      - name: Notify Success
        if: success()
        uses: actions/github-script@v6
        with:
          script: |
            github.issues.createComment({
              issue_number: 1,
              owner: context.repo.owner,
              repo: context.repo.repo,
              body: "OpenTofu deployment succeeded!"
            })
```

In this, the secrets are passed as variables to the OpenTofu plan command, ensuring they are injected securely without exposure.

Encrypting State files

The state files may contain sensitive information which needs secure encryption and safe storage too. We may do as below:

- Use Remote Backends with Encryption

Configure a remote backend like AWS S3 with encryption enabled.

```
# backend.tf
terraform {
  backend "s3" {
    bucket         = "opentofu-state-bucket"
    key            = "prod/terraform.tfstate"
    region         = "us-east-1"
    dynamodb_table = "terraform-state-lock"
    encrypt        = true
  }
}
```

Here, the **encrypt = true** setting ensures that the state file is stored securely using server-side encryption.

Integrating with HashiCorp Vault

In order to have advanced secret management, we can simply integrate OpenTofu with HashiCorp Vault. To do this,

- Store Secrets in Vault

First, we store your secrets in Vault using the CLI or API.

```
vault kv put secret/publishing_app/db_password
value="ProdSecurePass123!"
vault kv put secret/publishing_app/api_key
value="APIKEY1234567890"
```

- Configure Vault Provider

Set up the Vault provider in your OpenTofu configuration.

```
# providers.tf
provider "vault" {
  address = "https://vault.yourdomain.com"
  token   = var.vault_token
```

```
}
```

- Retrieve Secrets from Vault

Use data sources to fetch secrets from Vault.

```
# secrets.tf
data "vault_kv_secret_v2" "db_password" {
  mount = "secret"
  name  = "publishing_app/db_password"
}
data "vault_kv_secret_v2" "api_key" {
  mount = "secret"
  name  = "publishing_app/api_key"
}
```

- Use Retrieved Secrets in Resources

Reference the fetched secrets in your resource definitions.

```
# main.tf
resource "aws_db_instance" "publishing_db_prod" {
  ...
  password = data.vault_kv_secret_v2.db_password.data["value"]
  ...
}
resource "aws_instance" "publishing_backend_prod" {
  ...
  user_data = <<-EOF
              #!/bin/bash
              export
API_KEY=${data.vault_kv_secret_v2.api_key.data["value"]}
              EOF
  ...
```

```
}
```

Here, the OpenTofu fetches secrets from Vault dynamically. The access to Vault and the secrets is controlled via tokens and policies, enhancing security.

When you put these techniques into practice, you're setting a reliable foundation for your infrastructure as code practices. This helps protect your publishing application against potential security threats and makes sure you're following industry standards.

Integrating Third-Party Tools

Let's walk through an example of integrating OpenTofu with GitHub Actions to automate the deployment of our publishing application's infrastructure. We will cover setting up the workflow, securing secrets, and implementing best practices for automated deployments.

Previously, we have already setup the GitHub Secrets and the Workflow. After defining the workflow, we now commit and push it to your repository.

```
git add .github/workflows/deploy.yml
git commit -m "Add GitHub Actions workflow for OpenTofu deployments"
git push origin main
```

Testing the Automated Deployment

Next, we perform a test deployment. For this, we modify a configuration in the staging environment and push it to the **`staging`** branch.

```
git checkout staging
# Make changes to staging configurations, such as adding a new EC2 instance or updating security groups
git add .
git commit -m "Update staging configurations for testing"
git push origin staging
```

This action triggers the GitHub Actions workflow, which will apply the changes to the staging environment automatically.

Next, after validating changes in staging, merge them into the **`main`** branch to promote them to production.

```
git checkout main
git merge staging
git push origin main
```

This merge triggers the GitHub Actions workflow to apply the same infrastructure changes to the production environment automatically.

Handling Failures and Rollbacks

It is also noticed that automated deployments can occasionally encounter issues. So here, it's essential to have strategies in place to handle failures and perform rollbacks when necessary. Here, we first modify the workflow to include steps that handle failures gracefully, such as notifying the team or triggering rollback procedures.

```
- name: Notify Failure
  if: failure()
  uses: actions/github-script@v6
  with:
    script: |
      github.issues.createComment({
        issue_number: 1,
        owner: context.repo.owner,
        repo: context.repo.repo,
        body: "OpenTofu deployment to `${{ github.ref }}` 
failed. Please investigate."
      })
```

This step sends a notification if the deployment fails, allowing the team to take immediate action. This whole integration accelerates your development lifecycle and fosters continuous improvement and teamwork. If you adopt these advanced automation techniques, you will have more confidence and control over your publishing application's infrastructure. This will make it easier for your company to succeed, even when the technology landscape is changing.

Summary

To sum it all up, we looked into how to improve our infrastructure management by using automation, flexible configurations and secure secret handling. First, we looked at automating infrastructure updates, where you learned how integrating OpenTofu with CI/CD pipelines, especially GitHub Actions, made deployment processes faster and easier. This made sure that infrastructure changes were consistent and error-free, deployment cycles were sped up, and continuous integration and deployment practices were made easier.

Then, we moved on to Managing Secrets in Configurations where we learned to keep secrets safe. You saw how secrets are managed with AWS Secrets Manager or HashiCorp Vault, and how GitHub Secrets can be used in CI/CD workflows. And finally, Integrating Third-Party Tools (GitHub Actions) showed how to connect OpenTofu with GitHub Actions to automate deployments, validate configurations, and get real-time notifications, making it all more secure and reliable. Overall, this chapter gave us some great advanced techniques to create a secure, efficient, and scalable infrastructure through automation and best practices.

Epilogue

With "Infrastructure as Code with OpenTofu" coming to an end, I hope you feel like you have the skills to take your infrastructure management to the next level. This book has given you the basics of OpenTofu, showing how you can effectively replace Terraform to get more cost-efficient and flexible results when managing your cloud environments. With everything you've learned in these chapters, you've got the know-how to automate deployments, create dynamic and scalable resources and securely manage sensitive data in your configurations. You've also learned how to integrate OpenTofu with GitHub Actions to streamline your CI/CD pipelines, making sure that your infrastructure evolves along with your application code. You've got real-world skills here. You can put this stuff into practice right away to make solid infrastructure that boosts both performance and security.

When you start using OpenTofu, you'll see a whole bunch of possibilities. You'll be able to build infrastructures that are strong, can grow, and are easy to take care of without having to deal with too many costs. The hands-on examples in this book will help you apply what you've learned to real-world scenarios, boosting efficiency and innovation on your team and in your organization. As you keep going on your journey, remember that the principles of automation, security, and scalability are the cornerstones of effective infrastructure management.

Thanks for choosing this book

I'm excited to see how you'll apply these learnings to transform your infrastructure practices and contribute to a more efficient and open cloud ecosystem. May all your deployments be quick, your configurations safe, and your infrastructures strong.

Thank You

www.ingramcontent.com/pod-product-compliance
Lightning Source LLC
Chambersburg PA
CBHW080213170726
48282CB00030B/1103
9788197950438